17 Lists That Will
Change Your Life

17 Lists That Will
Change Your Life

THOUGHT CATALOG

BROOKLYN, NY

THOUGHT
CATALOG
Books

Cover Design: www.athleticsnyc.com

Published by Thought Catalog Books, a publishing house owned by The Thought
& Expression Co., Williamsburg, Brooklyn.

Second edition, 2018

CONTENTS

21 Ways You Should Take Advantage Of Your 20s

Sari Moon

1. Don't feel the need to respond to every text message, phone call, and email the second it reaches you. Once upon a time, it took longer than a minute to reach someone. People used stamps and envelopes; they had answering machines they didn't check for hours, sometimes days. No one will die if you don't immediately respond to every message you receive.

2. Ask for what's owed to you. Half the time, you're not getting your needs met because you're not making them known. Your employers, romantic interests, and friends are not going to read your mind and give you what you need unless you speak up.

3. Never turn down an open bar. Seek them out and make them a priority. Indulging in open bars when you're older isn't appropriate because a) people will

think you have an alcohol problem and b) you're supposed to have enough money to afford your own alcohol.

4. If you're unhappy and someone offers you a way out, take it. You don't owe your first job years of loyalty and your first-born; you don't have to stay in your city just because you're on a first-name basis with the bodega guy. Do what feels right; the initial fear will give way to excitement.

5. Take advantage of all the energy you have in your 20s. In your 30s and 40s, your body starts getting upset with you, when some 20-something babe is all, "Wanna race?" That's not a concern when you're in your 20s — don't ever take it for granted.

6. Let your more successful friends pick up the check this time. Before you're 30, it's still okay to be work as a barista and not have your career path figured out. Save your cash and take up your lawyer-friend's offer for dinner. Use the money you saved to buy more ramen.

7. Play a sport you played in elementary school. Kickball, dodgeball. There are leagues for these games now. Get on it.

8. Learn how to cook. Here's an idea — instead of spending all your money on ridiculously marked-up restaurant food, save your money by buying non-processed WHOLE FOODS and LEARNING HOW TO MAKE A MEAL OF REAL FOOD. A meal of real food is not a box of Annie's Organic Mac and Cheese — that's PROCESSED FOOD. A meal is

something like sautéed brussel sprouts with onions and pinto beans garnished with salt and pepper. You'll thank yourself for learning how to cook when your metabolism catches up to you.

9. Keep making friends. Everyone complains that it's hard to make friends after college, but we still manage to find new people to flirt with and date, right? It's not that hard. You know yourself better than you ever have before, and your friends can finally reflect that. Don't cling to old friends because it's too frightening or 'risky' to make new ones.

10. Let your parents buy your plane ticket home. It can be trying to be stuck in a house with your family for a few days or a week, but vacations in your 20s can be hard to come by. Let them subsidize your trips home and do you as much as you can when you get there.

11. Stay up late. In your 20s, you're all, "Let's go to another bar!" "Who wants to eat at a diner?" "Have you guys seen the sunrise from the High Line?" "In this moment I swear we were infinite!" When you get older, this becomes, "What are you doing? Go home. Watch Parks and Rec and go to sleep. What is wrong with you, staying up all night? Who has time for that?" If you're in your 20s, you do. You have all the time. Do it now and take advantage of how not tired you are. You think you're crabby now when you stay up too late? You'll never believe how terrible you feel when you do it in your 30s.

12. Savor those 20s hangovers. They are a gift from God

so that you'll always remember what your tolerance level is. Your hangover recovery time is like flippin' Wolverine in your 20s. You wake up, feel like death, pull on some shades, gulp down coffee or maybe a Bloody Mary and whine about your headache over brunch. Oh, boo hoo. When you're older, every hangover is Apocalypse Freaking Now. You're not making it to brunch. You're not making it off your floor in a weeping puddle of regret.

13. Indulge in diner/ fast food at 4 a.m. This is considered depressing behavior once you become a real adult.

14. STOP PROCRASTINATING YOUR TRIP ABROAD. YOUR CHANCES OF TAKING A LONG VACATION ABROAD DIMINISH AS YOU BECOME MORE SET IN YOUR WAYS AND AS YOU GAIN MORE RESPONSIBILITY.

15. Do 'unacceptable' things to your hair. Dye it. Dread it. Shave only the left side of your head and give a crap if it grows back in a flattering manner (hint: it won't). There's no time but now.

16. Avoid Burning Man. Save it for your weird-Dad mid-life crisis.

17. Sit down, unplug, and read non-fiction. Do this daily. None of your peers are doing it. They're playing video games and refreshing Facebook and Gmail chatting about nothing in particular. After a month you'll be smarter than all of them.

18. Walk into Forever 21 and grab every single

crappily-made floral dress available. Is every other girl on the street wearing it? Is it literally falling apart at the seams? Is it also actually five dollars? BUY IT IMMEDIATELY. When you get older, your clothing becomes all expensive blazers and tailored khakis and other pieces that won't break while on your body. That will be a great day — the day when your closet starts to look respectable. Though those outfits are more expensive, they also last longer and look better on you. You will be a classy human ready to take on the future. But as long as you're still in your 20s? You know — the demographics of Forever 21? Game on, stretchy black dress with pockets that lasts about a week. Game on.

19. Take road trips. Sitting in a car for days on end isn't something your body was designed to do forever.

20. Don't invest in things like window curtains or throw rugs or... Windex. You're a young, social person who doesn't have time for things like picture-framing and broom-sweeping. No one actually expects you to maintain a bed skirt or a duvet cover in your 20s, they're the home decor equivalent of puppies/children.

21. Go to/host theme parties. Once people age out of their 20s, no one's trying to wear pajamas or Saran Wrap out of the house. The only theme parties that exist after your 20s are 'Wedding,' 'Baby Shower,' and 'Funeral.'

2

15 Guaranteed Things That Will Happen To You in Your 20s

Ryan O'Connell

1. Your social circle will narrow. In college, you'll have lots of acquaintances and party friends but that will dissipate over time. Eventually, you'll find yourself unable to spark up new friendships simply because you don't have the time or desire. Now you'll only make a new friend and let them into your life if you're absolutely obsessed with them.

2. You'll seriously consider going to grad school. You'll call your mom up in a panic one day and explain that you've always enjoyed something like psychology and, well, maybe it's time to start entertaining the idea of, um, being a therapist. Mom? Stop sighing!

3. You will hate your job at some point, even if it's better than 99% of your other friends' jobs. You will be

overworked and underpaid presumably until you're 40. Then, you'll suddenly be overpaid and not do much of anything. Right? That's how it works?

4. Someone will betray your trust — a friend or a lover — and it will change the way you view people forever.

5. You will do things that hurt you just because you're not ready to feel good yet.

6. You will sleep with people who you genuinely like, have a great time with, but never want to date. Ever.

7. After learning your age, someone will say to you, "Wow, you're so young!" and occasionally you'll believe them.

8. You'll miss certain days before they even end.

9. You'll spend an entire day hungover in bed and nothing will make you feel more like a fucking idiot. Not even taxes or putting the fitted sheet on your bed.

10. You'll read a book that will change your life. People say that all the time, especially your grandma and your mom and your professors in college, and it always made you roll your eyes but now you get it. Life is changed. You are this book's bitch. You fell in love with it in the same way you fell in love with someone in high school: blindly and all-consuming. I'm talking about the book that became the lens through which you chose to see the world. You were just waiting for something to come along and explain to you how the world works, to make it all easier for you. and it came.

You will remember this book more vividly than some of the people you dated for three months in college.

11. You'll meet people who are vultures, who were literally sent to this world just to annoy you, to work half as hard and somehow become more successful. They're networking leeches. Don't take their business card! Save yourself!

12. Some days you will wake up and be astounded by how ugly you are. People are always saying things like, "OMG, I look like shit right now!" but they don't. You're the one who looks like shit (truly!) so shut up everyone else!

13. That being said, there'll be some days when you look in the mirror and think to yourself, "Okay, I'd fuck me." That's good. It's healthy to want to fuck yourself.

14. The Internet will hurt your feelings. You will find out information you wish you never knew and maybe you'll go so far as to even cry! Imagine that: a machine you spent over a grand on is making you weep. Screw the Internet.

15. You will understand that the biggest battle you fight in your twenties is the one you're in with yourself. The most important thing you can learn in this decade is how to love yourself. Without that knowledge, your life will always be a little bit terrible. You will always be dating someone who's a little bit rotten and you'll always be working a job that sucks. It affects everything so be sure to make yourself a priority. Work

on liking yourself before working on getting someone else to like you.

3

24 Rules For Living From A (Semi-) Successful 26-Year-Old

Ryan Holiday

I'm not saying I have everything figured out. In fact, I'm saying the opposite. My parents were good to me growing up, at least in terms of my physical well-being and my material wants. But the one thing I didn't get was advice. I don't recall many situations where my father took the opportunity to use a particular instance to give me general advice. Which of course, is the best way to learn about the world.

Now that I think about it, they didn't really teach much how to do a lot basic things either. I'm not talking about how to fix a flat tire or how to change your oil–you can pay someone to do that. This is embarrassing but I remember checking into my first hotel as an adult, during college probably, and getting assigned to room 1214 or something and actually thinking for a second: "How am I supposed to know what floor that's on?"

All I'm saying is that it would have been really nice if one of my parents, during the several dozen times we'd stayed in a hotel as a child, had taken two seconds to say, "Hey six year old, this is how this whole system works." You know, instead of hoping I observed everything (which in the case of the elevator thing, I probably should have but clearly did not).

That being said, I turned 26 this week and all things considered, I've done pretty well for myself. Stumbling and fumbling through the dark, I've managed to become a bestselling author, work for some pretty cool people, start my own company, not fuck up my relationship with a girlfriend I love, and for whatever reason, now people come to ME for advice.

I'm sure many of you will disagree with these rules and shortcuts. You'll say they're cheating or wrong or inefficient. You may be right. They are, after all, the rules of someone who is completely self-taught. All I can say is that they work.

[*] Talking about what you're going to do makes you a lot less likely to actually do it. Keep your plans to yourself.

[*] If it's less than 2 floors, never take the elevator. Take the stairs. Nassim Taleb talks about this too: Carry your own bags. Take the stairs. Walk instead of taking a cab. You were already planning to go to the gym later, don't be an idiot. Exercise is exercise.

[*] Always pull the car up to the very end of the curb (never waste a parking spot)

[*] Public speaking is only hard or scary if you don't think you know what you're talking about. That's relatively simple to fix.

[*] Never recline your seat on an airplane. Yes, it gives you more room–but ultimately at the expense of someone else. In economics, they call this an externality. It's bad. Don't do it.

[*] After you're done eating at a restaurant, just hand the waiter your card. You don't need to see the receipt first (99% of the time it's right and if it isn't–it's their fault. Send them back to fix it). Also, there's no need to calculate the tip. I just enter the final number I'm paying. I'm paying them, they can do the math for me. (Provided you actually tip well.)

[*] If someone wants to go faster, let them pass.

[*] When you're traveling to a new city, the first thing you should do when you get to the hotel is change into your work out clothes and go for a long run. You get to see the sights, get a sense of the layout and then you won't waste an hour of your life in a lame hotel gym either.

[*] Never correct someone's pronunciation of a word with the more appropriate ethnic accentuation. Only small people care that much about grammar or pronunciations.

[*] Everything your doctor, school and parents said was healthy is probably bad for you. Whole grains, soy, corn, wraps, milk. Ask yourself: does what I am about to eat even remotely resemble something my ancestors evolved to eat? If the answer is no, put it down. If, like me, the allure of these foods is too much, save them for one day a week where you splurge (and then hate yourself and swear them off for another week).

[*] Unless it's an atrocity, take responsibility for it. You're probably more at fault than you know.

[*] Get a dog, not a cat. One will make you a better person, the other is just an animal that lives in your house.

[*] In business situations, your first instinct is to start negotiating. Stop that. How much is significantly less important than whether you truly, truly want to do this thing. If you do–and I know this advice is controversial–just take the deal, provided its half way decent. Don't look a gift horse in the mouth. Bird in the hand. Blah blah. If you don't want to do it–don't let money sway you. Take the deal, do a good job, get more money on the next one. This is the philosophy of doers. Sharks and sociopaths care about squeezing every penny because they've confused money with their worth.

[*] Shame is a powerful emotion that can be used for good. If it's something you want to hide or are embarrassed about, think twice about whether it's actually the right thing. (Two good one-liners about this here).

[*] Be in the middle of a book at all times. Better still, carry one with you at all times–a physical one. You'll be amazed at how impressed people are by this.

[*] Frequent Flyer Miles are for people whose time is worthless. Here's what I do: I use a Southwest Visa card. It means I get a few extra free domestic flights a year without ever having to do anything. And then on everything else? I never, ever think about it–even though I fly close to 50,000+ miles a year. If I am going to have to juggle a bunch of arbitrary, meaning-

less numbers for piddly rewards, I'd rather juggle sports stats or play games on my cell phone. At least those are entertaining.

[*] Most people are lying when they describe what their life is like. Don't listen, don't use what they say as a baseline, don't get jealous, just nod and then forget it.

[*] Speaking of which, people are constantly trying to bribe you to be like them and take on the same burdens as them. DO NOT ACCEPT.

[*] Traveling for the sake of traveling is stupid.

[*] If there is a long line and you don't want to wait in it, walk up to the front (or walk through the back or opposite way) and pretend you didn't know you were doing things incorrectly. It almost always works. And when it doesn't, no one thinks it was malicious. After all, you were just turned around. Note: pretending you forgot something–like you were just walking up to grab silverware at the buffet line–works well too. Grab your stuff and make a getaway.

[*] The best way to flirt is to ask provocative questions. And provocative is anything people aren't expecting to be asked–it doesn't have to be sexual.

[*] Eliminate options, concentrate your forces. Here I am combining two lessons from Tim Ferriss and Robert Greene. For example, in terms of clothes and meals, just pick a few favorites and then stick with them. This means less time is wasted thinking about choices on a daily basis. But more importantly, concentrating your limited dollars/time on fewer

entities gives you more leverage. I mostly eat at the same restaurants over and over–and you know what, they always hook me up. The fastest way to VIP status on anything is to cheat by going or buying a few times in a row. There's a saying behind this too: More wood behind fewer arrows. It applies to more than just dinner perks.

[*] Conference calls and meetings are mostly a waste of time. If the person is more important or successful than you, consider going. If not, beg off as best you can.

[*] Current events/the news should be followed only if it fits one of the following criteria 1) It directly affects you in some way. 2) Knowing about it would make for interesting conversation. If you're watching something and you can't tell yourself that you either plan to do something with that information or it will make you seem smart, turn it off. Or flip it over to Comedy Central because you may as well be watching pure entertainment.

*****

This isn't conclusive. It's just some stuff that occurred to me and that I think about often enough to have a policy on. I don't think it's a coincidence that a lot of them line up with sayings or clichés. Those are clichés for a reason–namely that they're true for a lot of people and have been for a long time.

All I know is that I wish I hadn't figured them out on my own (or in some cases, heard from mentors and other smart people, but only well into my twenties.) Because missing these rules was painful. It wasted time, money and energy.

Hopefully they save you some trouble. And I guess, the message, at the end of the day, is that it's never too late.

4

30 Life Lessons For 20-Somethings With Too Many Feelings

Danielle Campoamor

1. Laugh constantly. Laugh freely. Laugh at every moment in your life. Laugh when it is appropriate. Laugh when it isn't. Laugh when it fucking hurts like hell. Laugh when the happiness escaping your throat is as smooth as a whiskey seven. If you cannot laugh when you're beat down. When you are hurt. When you are two seconds away from inhaling a pain that will drown you, you will never survive.

2. Orgasms are by far, hands down, the best thing for your complexion. Don't waste money on some ridiculously overpriced face wash. Lancome is a lie. So is Cover Girl. Instead, put your fingers to work. Go pay the thirty or fifty bucks for a bunny that's guaranteed to get you off. Become comfortable enough with an

individual to sleep with them on a daily basis. Just cum consistently and your pores will thank you.

3. A cob salad has more calories than a double cheeseburger. Don't kid yourself.

4. A girl can never own too many stilettos. Yes, they will hurt. Yes, they will cost almost as much as your rent. Yes, while they were once undeniably beautiful you will inevitably wreck them thanks to countless nights plagued with tequila and bad decisions. It doesn't matter. They will make you feel beautiful when you can't stand to look at yourself in the mirror. They will make your legs appear longer, your form appear slimmer, and your ass appear Brazilian.

5. Argue. Debate. Disagree. That is the only way you will become privy to the beauty that is an organic learning environment. Keep an open mind. Listen. Nod at the appropriate time. Stand up for yourself when necessary and shut the fuck up when you should. A coalition of different viewpoints is essential to true understanding. Be prideful enough to lend verve to your voice and humble enough to know when your voice is cracking.

6. Music will save you. It will also kill you. Certain songs will repair gaping holes in your heart while others will send you back two years ago; when you were in his arms, kissing his lips, and resting your head on his shoulders as he strangled his fingertips with your hair. Regardless, music is a constant reminder that it's okay to feel. It is okay to remember, to reminisce, and to

be sad. It's okay to cry laugh smile lose control scream dance become far too sentimental forget. To. Just. Be. Hiding behind intoxicating melodies and beautiful breakdowns is the universe's permission to feel. So close your eyes and turn up the volume.

7. Tequila will do one of two things. A) Make you fall in love with everyone. And I mean everyone. Or B) Make you ridiculously protective to an almost violent degree. You despise the man who gave your best friend a second glance. You automatically distrust the poor sap who offered to buy your roommate a drink. You are ready to throw down for their honor, dignity, and virginity. No, it doesn't matter that they lost it years ago.

8. Champagne will give you the worst hangover of your life.

9. Wine will make you wish you were Mormon.

10. Jäger will, without a doubt, make you do that one thing you boy-scout-honor-swore you'd never. Ever. Do.

11. Reading is pivotal. Another human being's syntax is the soul's water. While walking a mile in another's shoes is impossible, caressing a stranger's paperback spine is the closest you will ever get to fully understanding another human. So sink into a chair every once in a while. Sit outside in the sun. Cuddle up next to a lover. A window. A fireplace. Just read.

12. Don't you dare read on a damn Kindle. Your fingertips need to feel the pages. Your nose needs to smell the

pine sacrificed in the name of literature. Visit your library. You will feel intellectual, organic, and sexy.

13. It is okay to be alone. In fact, everyone should be at least once. Surround yourself in the silence that is independence. Stop looking for someone so that you may find yourself.

14. It is essential in one's life to experience a one night stand. The awkward morning-after will remind you that you aren't made for consistent promiscuity. The allure of a dirty night with a relative stranger will make you feel like Pamela incarnate.

15. Craigslist is the perfect example of both the rise and fall of society.

16. You are capable of handling situations you couldn't have possibly imagined. Fathers will disown you. The love of your life will sleep with someone else. The person who made you will hit you. Your best friends will die. A man will ignore your fervent "no" and take what he wants. And still you will find yourself filling your lungs when situations should have left them empty. It is in those moments that you'll remember there isn't anything you cannot overcome.

17. There isn't anything you will be capable of overcoming without your friends.

18. The cure for any discomforting situation or painful realization or heavy moment within one's life, is driving. Nothing will take away the feelings of failure like a never-ending road, a rolled down window, a

six-speed manual, a music collection of epic and speaker-destroying proportion, and (of course) a pack of cigarettes. Drive until you have left it all behind you. You will eventually have to return to it all, however the miles you've put between you and a rude reality will strengthen your resolve.

19. The ones you love the most will hurt you the most. Mothers will be incapable of protecting you when they should. The most important man in your life will hurl hurtful words in your direction. Best friends will write words dipped in resentment. You will reach out to someone in tears, scared and alone, only to have them decide it is too much and disappear. Forgive them instantly. Love them regardless. And know that you, despite your best efforts, have hurt them too.

20. Talk dirty in bed. Get over being uncomfortable and push past the urge to compare yourself to a mediocre porn star. While between the sheets with a fantastic lover, say everything you have ever wanted to say or do or have felt. Those words will assist you both in obtaining levels of pleasure previously believed to be nothing more than a filthy fairytale.

21. Slow dance. Don't leave your youth in a middle school gym.

22. Whatever you do, do not pass out on the bathroom floor of a gay bar. Enough said.

23. It is okay to ask for help. It is okay to swallow your pride, choke down your guilt, chew on your inadequacies, and realize that you cannot do

everything by yourself. Everyone needs help at one time or another. Including you.

24. You are not confined to the family God gave you. You have the beautiful ability to hand pick your own. College friends will become your sisters. Ex-boyfriends' fathers will become your own. Best friends of your brothers will become baby brothers one, two, and three. Cherish them, protect them, and allow them to do the same.

25. Enjoy having too much. Too much Jack Daniels. Too much love. Too much dancing. Too much work. Too much procrastination. Too much time. Too much responsibility. Too much insecurity. Too much coffee. Too much doubt. Too much of not enough. Realize that overindulgence is the key to neutrality. Realize that a painful destruction is essential to the construction of something wonderfully beautiful. So take one shot too many. Stay out until six-thirty, when you have to be at work at nine. Tell them that you love them, even when you know it is too much.

26. Girls poop. Yes, it can rival a man's in both stench and quantity. Get over it.

27. Make fun of yourself. When others do, it will help it hurt less.

28. Remember how blessed you are. You can be covered in bruises and overflowing with emptiness. You can be lost, alone, and fantastically hurt. However, it can always. Always. Be worse. And for countless others, it is. So after you have tended to your bruises and

replaced the smallest amount of emptiness with a tangible satisfaction. After you've been found and are standing next to another and your hurt has diminished. Be thankful.

29. Whoever said money doesn't buy happiness, lied. Sometimes, it takes money to find yourself at a concert with friends or three sheets to the wind or atop a needle sharing scenery with those that have never experienced it before. Pay for it anyways. Sign the check that makes your stomach turn. Eventually you will look back on those moments and realize that you would have paid twice that amount.

30. You can plan and scheme and write in a neat little notebook. You can create numerous lists that await the swift line of completion, but it won't matter. Nothing will end up the way you thought it would. Things will happen that you couldn't have possibly foreseen. Life doesn't care about the plan. The scheme. Your neat notebook. Or your fifty lists.

Including this one.

5

19 Things To Stop Doing In Your 20s

Brandon Gorrell

1. Stop placing all the blame on other people for how they interact with you. To an extent, people treat you the way you want to be treated. A lot of social behavior is cause and effect. Take responsibility for (accept) the fact that you are the only constant variable in your equation.

2. Stop being lazy by being constantly "busy." It's easy to be busy. It justifies never having enough time to clean, cook for yourself, go out with friends, meet new people. Realize that every time you give in to your 'busyness,' it's you who's making the decision, not the demands of your job.

3. Stop seeking out distractions. You will always be able to find them.

4. Stop trying to get away with work that's "good

enough." People notice when "good enough" is how you approach your job. Usually these people will be the same who have the power to promote you, offer you a health insurance plan, and give you more money. They will take your approach into consideration when thinking about you for a raise.

5. Stop allowing yourself to be so comfortable all the time. Coming up with a list of reasons to procrastinate risky, innovative decisions offers more short-term gratification than not procrastinating. But when you stop procrastinating to make a drastic change, your list of reasons to procrastinate becomes a list of ideas about how to better navigate the risk you're taking.

6. Stop identifying yourself as a cliché and start treating yourself as an individual. Constantly checking your life against a prewritten narrative or story of how things "should" be is a bought-into way of life. It's sort of like renting your identity. It isn't you. You are more nuanced than the narrative you try to fit yourself into, more complex than the story that "should" be happening.

7. Stop expecting people to be better than they were in high school — learn how to deal with it instead. Just because you're out of high school doesn't mean you're out of high school. There will always be people in your life who want what you have, are threatened by who you are, and will ridicule you for doing something that threatens how they see their position in the world.

8. Stop being stingy. If you really care about something,

spend your money on it. There is often a notion that you are saving for something. Either clarify what that thing is or start spending your money on things that are important to you. Spend money on road trips. Spend money on healthy food. Spend money on opportunities. Spend money on things you'll keep.

9. Stop treating errands as burdens. Instead, use them as time to focus on doing one thing, and doing it right. Errands and chores are essentially rote tasks that allow you time to think. They function to get you away from your phone, the internet, and other distractions. Focus and attention span are difficult things to maintain when you're focused and attentive on X amount of things at any given moment.

10. Stop blaming yourself for being human. You're fine. Having a little anxiety is fine. Being scared is fine. Your secrets are fine. You're well-meaning. You're intelligent. You're blowing it out of proportion. You're fine.

11. Stop ignoring the fact that other people have unique perspectives and positions. Start approaching people more thoughtfully. People will appreciate you for deliberately trying to conceive their own perspective and position in the world. It not only creates a basis for empathy and respect, it also primes people to be more open and generous with you.

12. Stop seeking approval so hard. Approach people with the belief that you're a good person. It's normal to want the people around you to like you. But it becomes a

self-imposed burden when almost all your behavior toward certain people is designed to constantly reassure you of their approval.

13. Stop considering the same things you've always done as the only options there are. It's unlikely that one of the things you'll regret when you're older is not having consumed enough beer in your 20s, or not having bought enough $5 lattes, or not having gone out to brunch enough times, or not having spent enough time on the internet. Fear of missing out is a real, toxic thing. You've figured out drinking and going out. You've experimented enough. You've gotten your fill of internet memes. Figure something else out.

14. Stop rejecting the potential to feel pain. Suffering is a universal constant for sentient beings. It is not unnatural to suffer. Being in a constant state of suffering is bad. But it is often hard to appreciate happiness when there's nothing to compare it to. Rejecting the potential to suffer is unsustainable and unrealistic.

15. Stop approaching adverse situations with anger and frustration. You will always deal with people who want things that seem counter to your interests. There will always be people who threaten to prevent you from getting what you want by trying to get what they want. This is naturally frustrating. Realize that the person you're dealing with is in the same position as you — by seeking out your own interests, you threaten to thwart theirs. It isn't personal — you're both just focused on getting different things that happen to seem mutually

exclusive. Approach situations like these with reason. Be calm. Don't start off mad, it'll only make things more tense.

16. Stop meeting anger with anger. People will make you mad. Your reaction to this might be to try and make them mad. This is something of a first-order reaction. That is, it isn't very thoughtful — it may be the first thing you're inclined to do. Try to suppress this reaction. Be thoughtful. Imagine your response said aloud before you say it. If you don't have to respond immediately, don't.

17. Stop agreeing to do things that you know you'll never actually do. It doesn't help anyone. To a certain extent, it's a social norm to be granted a 'free pass' when you don't do something for someone that you said you were going to do. People notice when you don't follow through, though, especially if it's above 50% of the time.

18. Stop 'buying' things you know you'll throw away. Invest in friendships that aren't parasitic. Spend your time on things that aren't distractions. Put your stock in fleeting opportunity. Focus on the important.

19. Stop being afraid.

6

25 Things To Do Before You Turn 25

Stephanie Georgopulos

1. Make peace with your parents. Whether you finally recognize that they actually have your best interests in mind or you forgive them for being flawed human beings, you can't happily enter adulthood with that familial brand of resentment.

2. Kiss someone you think is out of your league; kiss models and med students and entrepreneurs with part-time lives in Dubai and don't worry about if they're going to call you afterward.

3. Minimize your passivity.

4. Work a service job to gain some understanding of how tipping works, how to keep your cool around assholes, how a few kind words can change someone's day.

5. Recognize freedom as a 5:30 a.m. trip to the diner with a bunch of strangers you've just met.

6. Try not to beat yourself up over having obtained a 'useless' Bachelor's Degree. Debt is hell, and things didn't pan out quite like you expected, but you did get to go to college, and having a degree isn't the worst thing in the world to have. We will figure this mess out, I think, probably; the point is you're not worth less just because there hasn't been an immediate pay off for going to school. Be patient, work with what you have, and remember that a lot of us are in this together.

7. If you're employed in any capacity, open a savings account. You never know when you might be unemployed or in desperate need of getting away for a few days. Even $10 a week is $520 more a year than you would've had otherwise.

8. Make a habit of going outside, enjoying the light, relearning your friends, forgetting the internet.

9. Go on a 4-day, brunch-fueled bender.

10. Start a relationship with your crush by telling them that you want them. Directly. Like, look them in the face and say it to them. Say, I want you. I want to be with you.

11. Learn to say 'no' — to yourself. Don't keep wearing high heels if you hate them; don't keep smoking if you're disgusted by the way you smell the morning after; stop wasting entire days on your couch if you're going to complain about missing the sun.

12. Take time to revisit the places that made you who you are: the apartment you grew up in, your middle school, your hometown. These places may or may not be here forever; you definitely won't be.

13. Find a hobby that makes being alone feel lovely and empowering and like something to look forward to.

14. Think you know yourself until you meet someone better than you.

15. Forget who you are, what your priorities are, and how a person should be.

16. Identify your fears and instead of letting them dictate your every move, find and talk to people who have overcome them. Don't settle for experiencing .000002% of what the world has to offer because you're afraid of getting on a plane.

17. Make a habit of cleaning up and letting go. Just because it fit at one point doesn't mean you need to keep it forever — whether 'it' is your favorite pair of pants or your ex.

18. Stop hating yourself.

19. Go out and watch that movie, read that book, listen to that band you already lied about watching, reading, listening to.

20. Take advantage of health insurance while you have it.

21. Make a habit of telling people how you feel, whether it means writing a gushing fan-girl email to someone

whose work you love or telling your boss why you deserve a raise.

22. Date someone who says, "I love you" first.

23. Leave the country under the premise of "finding yourself." This will be unsuccessful. Places do not change people. Instead, do a lot of solo drinking, read a lot of books, have sex in dirty hostels, and come home when you start to miss it.

24. Suck it up and buy a MacBook Pro.

25. Quit that job that's making you miserable, end the relationship that makes you act like a lunatic, lose the friend whose sole purpose in life is making you feel like you're perpetually on the verge of vomiting. You're young, you're resilient, there are other jobs and relationships and friends if you're patient and open.

7

50 Awesome Quotes That Will Inspire You To Take That Risk

Chrissy Stockton

"If you do what you've always done, you'll get what you've always gotten."
TONY ROBBINS

"If you're offered a seat on a rocket ship, don't ask what seat! Just get on."
SHERYL SANDBERG

"I always did something I was a little not ready to do. I think that's how you grow. When there's that moment of 'Wow, I'm not really sure I can do this,' and you push through those moments, that's when you have a breakthrough."
MARISSA MAYER

"If you're going to be thinking anything, you might as well think big. Donald Trump Pearls don't lie on the seashore. If you want one, you must dive for it."

CHINESE PROVERB

"You can't outwit fate by standing on the sidelines placing little side bets about the outcome of life. Either you wade in and risk everything you have to play the game or you don't play at all. And if you don't play you can't win."
JUDITH MCNAUGHT

"If things seem under control, you are just not going fast enough."
MARIO ANDRETTI

"Do the one thing you think you cannot do. Fail at it. Try again. Do better the second time. The only people who never tumble are those who never mount the high wire. This is your moment. Own it."
OPRAH WINFREY

"Life is inherently risky. There is only one big risk you should avoid at all costs, and that is the risk of doing nothing."
DENIS WAITLEY

"Go out on a limb. That's where the fruit is."
JIMMY CARTER

"The universe has no restrictions. You place restrictions on the universe with your expectations."
DEEPAK CHOPRA

"Do one thing every day that scares you."
ELEANOR ROOSEVELT

"In order to succeed, your desire for success should be greater than your fear of failure."
BILL COSBY

"Your time is limited, so don't waste it living someone else's life."
STEVE JOBS

"If you are not willing to risk the unusual, you will have to settle for the ordinary."
JIM ROHN

"There is only one way to avoid criticism: do nothing, say nothing, and be nothing."
ARISTOTLE

"You get what you settle for."
THELMA AND LOUISE

"If you don't build your dream, someone else will hire you to help them build theirs." DHIRUBHAI AMBANI
"I refuse to accept other people's ideas of happiness for me. As if there's a 'one size fits all' standard for happiness."
KANYE WEST

"The first step toward success is taken when you refuse to be a captive of the environment in which you first find yourself."
MARK CAINE

"Always go with your passions. Never ask yourself if it's realistic or not."
DEEPAK CHOPRA

"You can't connect the dots looking forward; you can only connect them looking backward. So you have to trust that the dots will somehow connect in your future. You have to trust in something – your gut, destiny, life, karma, whatever. This approach has never let me down, and it has made all the difference in my life."
STEVE JOBS

"Leap and the net will appear."
ZEN SAYING

"I don't think you're human if you don't get nervous."
SIDNEY CROSBY

"A ship in harbor is safe, but that is not what ships are built for."
JOHN A. SHEDD

"Think big and don't listen to people who tell you it can't be done. Life's too short to think small."
TIM FERRISS

"I've missed more than 9000 shots in my career. I've lost almost 300 games. 26 times I've been trusted to take the game-winning shot and missed. I've failed over and over and over again in my life. And that is why I succeed."
MICHAEL JORDAN

"Your dreams are ballbusters; they're not the yellow brick road."
KELLY CUTRONE

"When you take risks you learn that there will be times when you succeed and there will be times when you fail, and both are equally important."
ELLEN DEGENERES

"If we listened to our intellect, we'd never have a love affair. We'd never have a friendship. We'd never go into business because we'd be too cynical. Well, that's nonsense. You've got to jump off cliffs all the time and build your wings on the way down."
ANNIE DILLARD

"When I let go of what I am, I become what I might be."
LAO TZU

"Only those who will risk going too far can possibly find out how far one can go."
T. S. ELIOT

"Don't be too timid and squeamish about your actions. All life is an experiment. The more experiments you make the better."
RALPH WALDO EMERSON

"Don't judge each day by the harvest you reap but by the seeds that you plant."
ROBERT LOUIS STEVENSON

"It is never too late to be what you might have been."
GEORGE ELIOT

"Often the difference between a successful person and a fail-

ure is not one has better abilities or ideas, but the courage that one has to bet on one's ideas, to take a calculated risk – and to act."
ANDRE MALRAUX

"Every man dies, but not every man really lives."
BRAVEHEART

"It is impossible to live without failing at something, unless you live so cautiously that you might have well not have lived at all, in which case you have failed by default."
J.K. ROWLING

"The best time to plant a tree was 20 years ago. The second best time is now."
CHINESE PROVERB

"Don't worry about failures, worry about the chances you miss when you don't even try."
JACK CANFIELD

"Twenty years from now you will be more disappointed by the things that you didn't do than by the ones you did do, so throw off the bowlines, sail away from safe harbor, catch the trade winds in your sails. Explore, Dream, Discover."
MARK TWAIN

"Everything you've ever wanted is on the other side of fear."
GEORGE ADDAIR

"Screw it, Let's do it!"
RICHARD BRANSON

"You can't have everything you want, but you can have the things that really matter to you."
MARISSA MAYER

"Trust your own instinct. Your mistakes might as well be your own, instead of someone else's."
BILLY WILDER

"I am thankful for all of those who said NO to me. It's because of them I'm doing it myself."
ALBERT EINSTEIN

"Only those who play win. Only those who risk win. History favors risk-takers. Forgets the timid. Everything else is commentary."
IVETA CHERNEVA

"And the day came when the risk to remain tight in a bud was more painful than the risk it took to blossom."
ANAIS NIN

"Life is being on the wire, everything else is just waiting."
KARL WALLENDA

"The question isn't who is going to let me; it's who is going to stop me."
AYN RAND

8

11 Life Hacks For The Emotionally Struggling 20-Something

Brianna Wiest

Everybody I know is either in or needs to be in therapy. The common theme among them is that they self-sabotage, and I think we all do, it's just that not all of us have the discipline to address it. I'm not one to pass judgment on this because I am guilty of it probably more than anyone, but I was able to figure some things out on the journey back from that place. I don't know your situation. I don't know what will help you. All I know is that these are the things I learned to hone in on every day and of which have brought me unprecedented happiness. By this I do not mean a sustained state of joy. I mean contentment; the ability to flow through emotions and the ins-and-outs and disappointments and numbing routines of everyday life; how to transcend them. How to garner your mindset to focus on a greater purpose, and to be able to have unfailing and even reckless faith and trust that the universe knows better than you do. Of course, getting to this place is a journey. I believe here is where you start.

1. You will not feel better tomorrow if you don't figure out what's wrong today. Tomorrow, and all the wonders the future can bring, is an illusion that is rooted in your mind's capability of deceiving itself into the idea that after a cycle of the earth's rotation things will be different. Less literally, if you can't enjoy what you have now, you are not in the right mindset to enjoy anything else. I'm sure you can attest to this in your own life as you see how the things you once lusted after, that are now yours, somehow seem ordinary and routine. It is because you received them without knowing how to enjoy them. If you want to break the cycle, start putting your energy toward reaching a nirvana state and embracing what is, and loving it for that. What's even greater about this is that the more you do so, the more you will see coming to you.

2. It's difficult to say goodbye in the digital age. You can't keep sending all of your time and energy into the black hole that is the unresolved and unwilling. More than that, with the rise of social media, it's increasingly difficult to not compare your life to other people's. Unfortunately, on these platforms, people are always presenting the bits and pieces of their lives that are incredibly fortunate and great. It makes that person feel better, and either annoys or makes everybody else feel substandard. It's a ruthless cycle, and you have to pluck yourself out of it.

3. You have to not only infuse your life with the little things that will make you enjoy your day, but also learn to free yourself from your thoughts that keep you in confines from enjoying said things. The major, overarching aspects of your life will always retreat to the background, and become the platform for your day. They will not be the things that capture your wonder and attention, this is reserved for the small miracles, and yes, they are miracles. It's the cliches, even, the cup of coffee and a book in bed on a Sunday morning, meeting an old friend for lunch, receiving a text or email from someone you love. Being able to touch someone's day and go home knowing you did something for this world. This is what life is about because your life could end in the next hour and these are the things you will have cherished.

4. Your life won't change in a day. Mindfully incorporate "healthy" practices into your life until they become routine. Please note, that by saying "healthy" I'm not trying to preach that you should run a half marathon every three months and only eat Paleo. I mean learn to breathe deeply. Learn to recognize the difference between your physical body and the person who inhabits it. The latter is who you really are. Drink water, you need it. Move and use the senses you were given: walk, read, speak, stretch. You won't always be able to.

5. Re-teach yourself how to feel. You're often too molded by your past experiences to go forth in the best way possible. Fighting those things is what gives them their

power. So you're sad today. It will pass. Appreciate why you're sad. It means you care enough about something to feel badly about it. Don't devalue or write off your emotions, they only have to be felt to be valid. It doesn't matter how "silly" it is or inconsequential whatever you are upset over is. Learn to apply this mindset to other people as well. Stop belittling people for what they do and don't feel. Realize that even though experiences are different, what we feel pertaining to them usually aren't. It's when we become numb that we really have a problem.

6. When you reach the point that you can appreciate the wonder in every one of your feelings, you will start realizing that there is more to life than just "happiness." Every part of it has its wonders. What's better than "happiness" is fascination, and interest, and commitment to maintaining light and love within yourself. Every situation is dimensional, and when you start realizing the possibility in any given situation, you will start understanding what it means to be alive.

7. I think that when people say "be grateful" and "appreciate what you have" they are entirely neglecting the fact that doing so is incredibly difficult when you're not in the mindset that appreciates anything whatsoever. In my experience, it's best to focus on one thing at a time. Be mindful of what your life would be like if you didn't have that thing. Your eyesight, a home, etc. I think it's far more effective to consider what life would be like without something than to just

acknowledge that not everybody is privileged in that way. You have to go deeper.

8. Vulnerability may be the most underestimated human experience. Don't be afraid to say you messed up, people will always be more understanding of those who admit their faults than of those who pretend as though they don't have any. There's an unprecedented opportunity for connection when people unapologetically admit to their human condition.

9. Although people's opinions shouldn't matter, they do, and may always, so it's better to figure out a way that you can filter what people are saying, try to see if they have anything of value to offer, but always be grounded in your own beliefs. Always. We will probably always be at the whim of our innate need for the love and acceptance of others. Instead of fighting that fact and pressing the idea that nobody else's ideas matter, we're better off figuring out how we feel first, and then trying to understand where someone is coming from if they say something that is less-than-pleasing to hear. The truth is, it's usually rooted in their own dissatisfaction.

10. Know that this path will not be easy. Nothing worthwhile, genuinely changing or in the human experience ever is. That's okay. It all serves a purpose far greater than your immediate satisfaction. We live in a culture that has built its foundations on the concept of instant gratification in the physical, material sense. Following and subscribing to this philosophy only pulls us farther and farther from our

natural states. It's difficult, yes, because it surrounds us. But you will continue in your cycle of discontentment until you learn otherwise. Often, the catalyst of this becoming is something traumatic, and what is produced in the aftermath shows us why our lives are infused with just the right amount of "misfortune." In a more beautiful phrasing than I could ever write:

"I think that we are like stars. Something happens to burst us open, but when we burst open and think we are dying; we're actually turning into a supernova. And then when we look at ourselves again, we see that we're suddenly more beautiful than we ever were before." — C. JoyBell C.

11. Sometimes you will be overcome with emotion, so much so that you feel as though you are panicking and you can't move on. Sometimes you don't even know why you feel the way you do, or you can't understand why something so mundane would evoke such a reaction. It is because when it comes to our feelings, there is always more than what meets the surface. This is not so with our thoughts, and that is where the confusion comes in. There are two things that everybody has to learn in this regard and it's how to let them infiltrate, overcome you, and then gently pass, and how, afterward, to dig into what it is that you are really upset about. Deal with that issue. It may be as simple as changing your mindset or as complicated as changing your lifestyle.

9

29 Eye-Opening Facts About Dating That Will Change The Way You View Relationships

Nico Lang

Being single again for the first time in a hot minute, I decided to do some research on the world out there that awaits us lonely wanderers — what the dating experts say on relationships. In doing so, I uncovered some interesting, alarming and a couple sadly unsurprising statistics. Some of them confirmed awful fears (and made the feminist in me cringe) and others made me want to hi-five a million angels.

I don't personally agree with all of these things (and some of it's a little dubious to me), but here's what the "experts" say about dating. As they say, knowledge is power:

1. You can't put a timeline on a relationship, and there's no telling when exclusivity is right for you, but according to a study from Lisa Daily, most couples get into an "exclusive" relationship after 6 to 8 dates.

2. Daily's study also suggests that men know when they're falling for someone as soon as three dates in. Women take longer, reporting the same feelings around date 14. Interestingly, that's exactly the same time that most couples say they exchange keys to each other's homes: between the 12th and 14th date.

3. Singledom is inertia. According to a commonly cited statistic from Neil Clark Warren, over half of people who report their relationship status as "single" say they haven't been on a date in two years. There's potentially a reason for this. When polled, 40% of men say that they are "scared" when first interacting with a potential mate.

4. Deciding whether you want to be in a relationship with someone is a protracted, often excruciating process of tests and feats of physical strength, like Heracles' labors or a holiday at home with your parents. However, knowing whether you want to have sex with someone is much simpler. According to Psychologists at UPenn, most people say they know within the first three seconds if they would fuck someone or not.

5. They say that most of communication is non-verbal, and "they" are right. Most women (57%) said that their first impressions of a guy are based off of his body language and self-presentation. Just 38% judged him on how he speaks and a low 7% cared about what he actually said. So, basically, women and men aren't that different after all.

6. Of course, body type matters in attracting a mate, but being "too skinny" counts against you much less than being overweight. Although overweight people are viewed highly unfavorably (even amongst children), people are more likely to ascribe positive characteristics to skinny people. According to Victoria Zdrock, they are often seen as "intelligent," although "fearful," as if every thin person were Woody Allen.

7. Although cultural norms suggest that men should always do the asking, Match.com polling reports that 91% of men who use the site are comfortable with a woman asking them out. Suck on that, patriarchy.

8. As far as who pays, Match suggests that increasing amounts of Americans are eschewing the traditional rule that the man pays for the first date. Between 2010 and 2012, the number of people who said that whoever did the asking should do the paying shot up from 21% to 32%, a 50% increase in just two years.

9. During the same time period, women were increasingly initiating nookie — because, hey, they're horny, too. In 2010, just over a third of women said that they would make the first move, but last year, almost half reported taking that initial baby step.

10. According to AskMen.com, Italian and Chinese food are favorites on dates, although Italian may be best prepared at home. They recommend Sushi for a second or third date and more adventurous choices like Moroccan or Ethopian for later dates, when you know if they would be into that sort of thing. (This

is how you know you have a keeper.) Greek is best consumed on a double date.

11. There's a particular reason for the no Greek rule or Ethiopian rule: They aren't great on the mouth, a huge deal for singles. When meeting a partner, two of the biggest considerations – commonly cited across gender lines — are the cleanliness of their teeth and the freshness of their breath. Next time, dudes, pop an Altoid before that date. Another big turn off is negativity, so smile when you do it.

12. According to Victoria Zdrock (aka Dr. Z), women said that ten of their biggest turn-offs were farting/burping, unkempt cuticles, nose hair, bad taste in eyeglasses, bad hair, acne, "man boobs" and when their date is missing a tooth. However, Betty White is missing a lot of teeth and seems to be doing fine, so I guess it's not transferrable across age and gender.

13. In more gender fuckery, women are more likely than men to say that they need independence in a relationship. Women report much higher needs of personal space, with 93% saying its very important to them, compared to 81% of men. While 63% of men say that they need their own finances in a serious relationship, a much higher 77% of women affirm that they want to keep those bank accounts separate.

14. In statistics that make me more sad, one study says that a woman will up her likelihood of divorce by 5% for every $5000 dollars she earns over her husband's salary. But if it ended badly, she might win in the

end. Research has shown that divorce is a killer —
shortening male life expectancy by almost 4 years.

15. Should a couple break up, the average breakup time
is between the three and five month period, when
things are just starting to get serious. Most breakups
are announced on a Monday, because what could be
worse than going back to work, amirite?

16. If you date online, you can often expect to break up
online. According to the Match singles, 48% of their
breakups took place over email. Luckily, though, only
5% of total breakups occurred over text message.

17. Although you can meet someone just about anywhere,
workplace relationships have a strangely high success
rate — if your goal is to put a ring on it. Around 40%
of romances that start at the water cooler result in
marriage. So make sure to wear that freakum dress to
your next office party ladies. Beyonce is watching.

18. If you live in New York or Washington and are looking
for love, you may be in luck. According to 2009 Census
stats, those two states have the highest percentages
of singles — with Washington reporting a whopping
70%. But Idaho has the highest rate of married folks
at 60%. Utah is close behind at 59%. Insert your jokes
here.

19. Also, you know how those girls on Sex and the City
always complained about how there were so many
single women but so few single men? That might be
true, as the Census suggests. Nationally there are 86
eligible males for every 100 women. However, there

are 100 million single people in the US, so one of them has to work out — at least I hope.

20. Side fact that I have no proof to back up: For the gays in the audience, there are 100 bottoms for every top. This isn't true, even though it could be, but goddamn it feels that way sometimes.

21. A survey in Glamour Magazine found that most women don't want to buy sex toys online. 66% preferred to do it in person, like shopping for a new dress or a clutch. 61% of those women said the reason was that they found the experience of buying it to be a turn-in in and of itself. The part where your vibrator thrusts inside you all night is just an added, wonderful bonus.

22. As far as sexual fantasies go, ABC reports that the most common is having sex outside — with a whopping 57% of the population saying they're into that. Only 14% of folks have had a threesome, but 21% of them have thought about it. (IMO, that means 86% of people need to have threesomes.) Less than a fifth of people have cheated on their partner, but much more of them have fantasized about doing so: Almost a third. Just over half of Americans say that they discuss these fantasies with their partners.

23. 48% of women say that they have faked an orgasm. 52% of women are liars. 25% of women will never achieve orgasm through sexual intercourse alone. The other 75% better have partners who will go down on them — or 100% of those men should be single.

24. In weird facts that seem apropros of nothing, a majority of women report being attracted to men who dress in blue on the first date. Too bad about that Blue Power Ranger then. All the good ones are gay — right, ladies? Except for Bradley Cooper. I hold out hope.

25. Men often say that they like the natural look on a woman, but they're dirty fucking liars. A memorable segment on Girl Code argued that "natural" for most men is Kim Kardashian, because they don't think she's wearing any makeup. And research shows that a) Kim Kardashian is wearing a ton of fucking makeup and b) men like that anyway. TLC and Chemistry.com found that a woman in a bar will be approached an average of six minutes more quickly if she's painted up.

26. According to the same set of statistics, men like their women to be "60 pounds lighter" than they are. Maybe it's a good thing I don't usually date women — because by that measure, I would be dating skeletons and children.

27. Although we think that queer people are more into "hookup culture" than their het counterparts ("the gay lifestyle," or whatever that means), that's actually not true at all. Queer folks (all those on the LGBTQ spectrum) are more likely to report that "romance" is most important to them in a relationship. The rates are 38% for gay men, 36% for lesbians and 32% for overall single people.

28. Be careful what you're sharing over the technology. According to Match.com, 48% of women and 38% of

men say that they research someone online before they go out with them, and similar numbers state that they would flake on a date because they found something they didn't like. If you're sexting with your date, like a majority of the population do, know that almost a quarter of people say that they show them to other people. So be mindful when sharing nudes.

29. Lastly, we're told that being in a relationship and being single are completely different, but those ol' Match.com statistics show that's not the case. Single people go out just as often as partnered folks do. When asked if they're out 1-3 times each week, 52% of singles said yes, and the figure for relationshippers was nearly identical (46%). So, single people, don't let anyone tell you that the grass is greener on the other side. That grass still gets shitfaced and makes stupid decisions at the bar, just like you do. Booze is the great equalizer.

10

7 Things That Happen To You When You Are Completely Honest

James Altucher

I got a death threat last week from a guy who's a senior at Brown University who didn't think I could track him down. More on that in a second. The first thing I want to deal with is the question asked me the other day: "How do you make a personal brand?" When I hear the words "personal brand," I think "someone is going to lie to me and then try to take all my money." Personal branding, I guess, is descended from the mockery called "corporate branding."

The Coca-Cola company, for instance, loves the drug Ecstasy. My favorite TV commercial is not the 1984 Apple commercial (although that's a close number two), but a commercial for Coke Zero ("Coke Zero Roller Girl"). It takes a song that was originally written by Paul Oakenfold. The original topic of the song was about how great it was to take the drug Ecstasy and go to a rave. Anything could happen.

There would be pretty girls, great music, and at the end of the night, total communion with nature. In the commercial, though, there's a girl rollerblading. She looks like she's on the boardwalk in Santa Monica. The song is playing in the background. She's not taking Ecstasy but drinking Coke Zero. She dances/rollerblades around her studly friends, her beautiful girlfriends, and it ends with everyone taking Coke Zero, the fizz going up like a group ejaculation into the sky. Coke Zero – the brand where you can find your own personal ecstasy.

I WANT THAT

Whenever I watch that commercial I feel like I want a life like that: free from worry, stress, free from thinking about money or petty jealousies. Surrounded by friends and beautiful people. Moving without effort, the ocean in the background. As they say in the song: "Once again, I find myself with my friends." Coke Zero tells me the dream is possible, even though intellectually I know it's a myth. Freedom isn't found that way. But we're willing, as a culture, to accept the lies Coke tells us. And they're willing to use songs about drugs to help us accept those lies.

Perhaps Coke figured out that maybe this time they had gone too far, because they pulled the commercial. Sometimes I can find it on YouTube. Sometimes I can't. They try hard to make it disappear.

What they never explain is that Coke Zero is essentially brown-dyed water with about 16 teaspoons of fake sugar in it. Add a little bit of CO_2 and you make it fizz. That's the secret formula that's locked in a safe in some bank in Atlanta. I can make SuperJamesCola with that formula. But then I can't license that music, get those sexy girls, and run that ad during the Super Bowl and a thousand other places. I can't do corporate branding by myself.

But no matter – let's move past the artificially safe confines of corporate America. That's dead and if you haven't planned your exit strategy yet you will have to soon enough.

SO WHAT IS PERSONAL BRANDING?

So now I keep hearing about "personal branding" – the idea that your career, your mind, your body, everything that makes up the superficial "you" can be packaged up into a brand just like Coke or McDonald's can. With the spectrum of pornography allowed by Facebook, Twitter, LinkedIn, Google+, etc. etc. etc., a personal brand can evolve and grow like any Superbowl ad. Kim Kardashian's didn't have an answer when Barbara Walters asked her, finally, "But aren't you really just known for a sex tape?" when Kim initially tried to "re-brand" herself as a "businesswoman" in a very intimate interview.

So we start to arrive at the truth of the matter: Branding is lying.

But personal branding is even worse because the joke is over. Now we're talking about me and you. We're talking about who YOU are. And let's face it. It's not pretty. You need to re-brand from birth.

People confuse "honesty" with a type of "happiness." He can be honest because he is happy. But it's not true. Life is a series of failures punctuated by brief successes. That's honesty. Failure is not necessarily bad. It's reality.

But branding tries to reverse that. With a "personal brand," you suddenly pretend to be super successful, a "business-woman" in Kardashian's case – failure is non-existent, and out of your mind comes the exact mathematical formulas that if someone drinks your Cola and snorts your Ecstasy, then they too will have the pretty girl, the success, the money, the accoutrements.

A FRIEND OF MINE WHO DOES PERSONAL BRANDING

I know a stockbroker who sends a Christmas card every year to his clients. He wants to present an aura of success. Each time he's in some other blue lagoon on some random part of the world, with a blonde girl (different each Christmas) with huge fake breasts and they are snorkeling or hugging in the water (blue blue aqua) or staring off into a beautiful Mediterranean ancient city. He makes money. Lots of it.

And you can't even look at him, the girl is so beautiful and her eyes are staring at him and she's kissing him and it's all over his Facebook page. His status might even be "engaged" and she has an exotic name.

The only problem is, "and you can't tell anyone because this is the beautiful part," he is telling me in his tell-all voice because he's a good friend and knows I will never reveal his name: is that he's gay. He picks up his boyfriends in dungeons. He's been smothered in concrete until he was unable to move and holes would be poked through so he could breathe, and only then with a boy whipping him and arranging this unusual punishment would he be able to finish.

*****

Honesty is about the scars. It's about the blemishes. But it's more than just bragging about failure, which could be a form of ego. It's about truly helping people.

There are a trillion websites competing against each other. The most honest website of all? Google. Google can't help you with your problems. If you suspect you might have herpes after a particularly courageous night out on the town, going to Google will not help you (although you may feel a vague feeling of remorse when you see the "I'm Feeling Lucky" button).

Google has no content on it at all. But Google is honest about that. You just walked into their store and said, "Please, help me – do you have anything to prevent a potential outbreak of herpes," and Google will say, quite honestly, "I'm sorry, I can't help you, but here are ten of my competitors who can potentially help you. And, by the way, here are three more of my competitors who MIGHT be able to help you, but, in full disclosure, they are paying me to tell you this." And then Google shrugs its shoulders. That's all they can do for you.

But that's honesty. That's not branding. So you'll come back to them. Because they are a straight shooter and the target was on your head. And when you need to know about that growth behind your ear, or what the best software is for keystroke logging, they will say the same thing: "Sorry, we can't help you – but we can direct you to at least ten of our competitors who seem pretty decent at it."

With honesty, they've set themselves free. Here's the thing about a brand. It puts you in jail. You know who had the original patent that Larry Page tweaked into the PageRank that made Google (and separately, that Robin Li ALSO tweaked into the patent that became Baidu?) I'll tell you: Dow Jones.

The Wall Street Journal. [See, "10 Unusual Things About Google"]

They knew how to make Google years before Larry Page even thought of the idea. But they didn't do it. Why? Because their brand says they don't give out stuff for free. Their brand says that everything you need to know is trapped inside something with the Wall Street Journal or Dow Jones trademarks printed on it and if it's not there then it's not anywhere. Branding jails corporate America but honesty sets entrepreneurs free.

WHAT WILL HONESTY GET YOU?

1. PEOPLE WILL STOP SPEAKING TO YOU

Forget personal branding. Start to dip your toes into personal honesty. Let me tell you what will happen. Your family might stop speaking to you. I have experienced this not just from myself but all the bloggers I consider "honest bloggers." Some of your friends will also stop speaking to you. Some of your colleagues will avoid you. Some investors will shun you. Your personal "network" will transform and shift. My own personal motto is: honesty to a point. I will never harm anyone. I believe in what Buddha said to his son Rahula the day after he showed up after abandoning his son for 7 years: "Before, during, and even AFTER you say something, make sure it doesn't hurt anyone." But even despite that rule, people will stop speaking to you because not every hurt you can control. Historical is hysterical for many people.

2. PEOPLE WILL THINK YOU ARE GOING TO KILL YOURSELF

The next thing that will happen is people will ask "Are you killing yourself?" Because every blog post almost seems like a suicide note.

3. PEOPLE WILL THINK YOU ARE CRAZY

Then people will send emails to your friends, "Is he as crazy as he sounds?" And that's how I make friends now because introductions will be made and people will have to find out for themselves.

4. PEOPLE WILL GET FRIGHTENED

So they will call you names. Oh, that guy is just trying to be a "contrarian," for instance. Or an "idiot." Or worse. I've been called everything. I had to call the Brown University Public Safety office the other day because I got emailed a death threat and the guy didn't think I could track him. The guy was a senior and had also apparently threatened the life of a librarian there. They need to understand why you are telling the truth. Why you are being honest about what you really think. In meetings at the office, everyone is quiet. You're not supposed to speak up. So people will dislike you, try to put you down, post comments, whatever. In many cases (but not all) these are what I call "crappy people". And here's how to deal with them.

5. PEOPLE WILL FIND YOU ENTERTAINING

Then finally, people will come back to you. Because you're entertaining – if 20,000 people are lying and only 1 person is telling the truth, then that 1 person is going to stand taller than anyone. At first people will come back to you for voyeuristic reasons. Why? Because they know if they watch Real Housewives they aren't watching anything "Real" and they aren't watching "Housewives." But you're real. So they want to know what you'll do next.

6. PEOPLE WILL TRUST YOUR ADVICE

People will also come back for advice. Not always because they agree with you. But because they know the advice is coming from the heart and not because there is anything for sale. It's like Google can't cure anything. But they can direct you to all the people who can. So you go back to Google because you might not always find what you want but at least you know they are trying hard to direct you to the right place. We've all hidden our failures in dark comets orbiting the peripheral edges of the solar system, where the sun is dark and faded. But when someone brings their orbit close to the sun we want to land there for a brief moment and see if actual living conditions exist. And if so, then maybe a small settlement can be formed, advice can be asked, a failure can be related to, a friendship can be formed.

7. YOU BECOME FREE

At first we hug our boundaries in chains. We think "If we tell the girl we like her, she might not like me back." We think, "If I say I like this candidate, my friends might hate me." If I say X, everyone else might say Y. And so on. But more and more we start to feel where those boundaries are and we push them out. We push them further and further away from ourselves. Until finally they are so far away it's as if they don't exist at all. You don't need money for that. Or a big house. Or a fancy degree or car. Every day, just push out those boundaries a little further. We reach for that freedom. We never truly get there. We're always striving to see how far they can go, just like a little child with her parents. But eventually, the boundaries are so far away we begin to feel the pleasures of true freedom.

And it feels good.

11

7 Things Girls Talk About Over Drinks

Chelsea Fagan

While my favorite activity in life is clearly making sweeping generalizations about strangers based on my own flawless experience, I am aware that not every one of the 3.5 billion women on this planet have conversations about dildos whilst sipping vodka with their respective juices.

1. **People we hate at work.**

   There is always at least one girl in the group who has someone at the office who is just gunning for her for no discernible reason. There are always several plot holes in these stories, but we ignore them just as we expect them to be ignored for us when we are bitching about that Terrible Work Person. This person is just evil, and usually unattractive in a naked mole rat sort of way (though we can never be sure how much of this element is projected), and has only one joy in life: making your friend miserable over shit as petty as the three-hole punch. It's the moment where all of the long-pent-up rage over leaving mystery Tupperware in the community fridge for weeks on end can spill out over your drinking friends like used motor oil, and everyone will nod faithfully in agreement.

2. **Sex, in the worst way possible.**
    We give men a lot of shit for how much they focus on sex, and that undoubtedly has more than a few grains of truth to it, but it's time to own up to the kind of chillingly graphic sex talk that occurs after a few drinks at a table full of women. You have to have that one fearless girl who leads the rest of the group like a noble sherpa through the mountains of dildo options and the pros and cons of using a finger in the butthole during a blowjob. This is the opportunity for everyone to A) recoil in horror at the things that they've never done with a dainty "Oh my god I could NEEEEVER" or B) offer up some hilarious tidbit about their partner's proclivity for getting smacked in the face during orgasm. The best part of all of this, it should be noted, is a few days later when you actually have to see this dude with your new, vivid knowledge of his private life and pretend that you are none the wiser.

3. **The fact that we're talking about girly shit.**
    If there is not that meta moment where you look at each other and go, "We are like an unfunny parody of Sex and the City right now. We are literally talking about nail polish and oral sex." the night is not yet over.

4. **Medical issues.**

   It's like WebMD but completely uninformed and mostly centered around the vague pains you are all experiencing around your back area. There are many theories, ranging from "birth control side effects" to "too much time on the elliptical" to "sleeping on a shitty Ikea mattress," all of which probably carry a degree of truth to them. The point, though, is that no one is going to be there to help you. (With the possible exception of the one girl who is a walking gynecological pharmacy and can tell you what the precise side effects of every form of contraception are, if you are in the market for such knowledge. She's had everything from the Nuva Ring to the patch to that one pill that causes heart attacks, and she has opinions to share.)

5. **Our exes, even though we are clearly with new people for some time now.**

   Especially if the ex is a mutual friend/acquaintance, there is truly never a bad time to recall all of the reasons you removed that loser from your life like some kind of remora who is incapable of keeping more than ten dollars in their checking account. If there has been a recent development in their douchiness made public via Facebook, it can provide hours of holier-than-thou fun for the whole family.

6. **Periods.**

   Yes, stupid men who make jokes about women all getting together and talking about their periods, I am giving you ammunition for your petty misogyny by admitting that sometimes women do in fact discuss the various nuances of the TIME WHEN THEY BLEED PROFUSELY FROM THEIR VAGINAS FOR SEVERAL DAYS OUT OF THE MONTH LIKE COME ON THIS IS A BIG ASPECT OF OUR LIVES WHY IS IT WEIRD THAT WE WOULD DISCUSS THIS FROM TIME TO TIME???? So shoot me that sometimes we're having cramps and want to know if anyone has any tips or a tampon or some ibuprofen. I'm sure that if you bled from your penis EVEN ONCE it would be literally the only thing you ever talked about. We would have national holidays celebrating your martyr status as the one who has to suffer the stigmata of human procreation. I truly cannot even find a fuck to give about your judgment.

7. **The agony and the ecstasy of ordering some mozzarella sticks.**
   Unless one of you steps up and goes straight for the buffalo wings right at the beginning (and God bless that person), there is going to be some completely superfluous hemming and hawing about whether or not you should all get a lil' something to snack on. God damn you, beauty industry, for making us feel like we have to justify the order of a plate of nachos with a comment on how bad it is or how we're going to run tomorrow or how we've been responsible all week. (The order may even trip the wire of a twenty-minute conversation on workout tips and/or kale chips and how they're really not so bad.) It's worth noting, though, that even though it will take the one girl brave enough to order on everyone else's cowardly behalf,

the second that plate of potato skins hits the table, it's getting swarmed upon like a plague of locusts, including by the girl who just got off a tirade about how much she's really into yoga and eating clean these days. Let's just own it, girls, we want those teriyaki chicken poppers, and no one is fooled into thinking we don't. Those poppers are wonderful, and so is being alive. Let's order the sampler.

12

44 Everyday Phrases You Might Not Know You've Been Saying Incorrectly

Nico Lang

After my last post on "words you might not know you've been saying incorrectly," a number of commenters posted that they often hear the same sense of malapropism applied to phrases. American English is full of idioms, as the language changes with everyday use, and these are just some of the phrases that vary by region, class and cultural background. All of them have become "accepted" over time, but many of them started out meaning something very different (see: #35). Some of them are just plain wrong and will be until the end of time (like #5). Others are just hilarious (#6).

Here are 44 common phrases that you might be saying or using wrong, some of which I weren't clear on until researching this article (#34). Which common malapropisms or abused phrases bother you? Leave your own grammar pet peeves in the comments.

1. Saying it wrong: "Chester drawers"
Doing it right: "Chest of drawers"
Despite what my mother thinks on the issue (who is a staunch defender of the malapropism), you do not own drawers that belong to Chester. If you do, you may want to give them back. A dresser is literally a chest made of out drawers, and the right way just makes a lot more sense. Sorry, Mom.

2. Saying it wrong: "For all intensive purposes"
Doing it right: "For all intents and purposes"
If something is intensive, that indicates that it's rigorous and focused, as it comes from the word "intense." Thus, you could have an intensive purpose if that entailed getting Ryan Gosling to marry you (because who doesn't want that), but it's not the same thing as "for all intents and purposes." If you were to say "Ryan Gosling and I are married "for all intents and purposes," you would be basically married or as our friends at Cambridge put it, married "in all the most important ways."

3. Saying it wrong: "Statue of limitations"
Doing it right: "Statute of limitations"
If you need some help with this one, turn to Seinfeld. Let Kramer be your guide of what not to do.

4. Saying it wrong: "I could care less"
Doing it right: "I couldn't care less"
"I could care less" doesn't make a lot of sense as a phrase. To be an appropriate put down, you want to indicate that you have no fucks left to give and your esteem is at its lowest possible level. Thus, if you're saying "I couldn't care less," it means

exactly that. It is impossible for you to give less of a shit about this.

5. Saying it wrong: "Warshing machine"
Doing it right: "Washing machine"

You cannot put something in a "warshing machine," because it doesn't exist. You also cannot go to "Warshington" or "Warshington D.C." Like "sherbet," you're adding an "r" where it doesn't need to be. However, try explaining this to people back where I'm from. Kentucky and Southern Ohio, drop those "r"s.

6. Saying it wrong: "Suppository of information"
Doing it right: "Repository of information"

This is my favorite malapropism ever, and allegedly once used by ex-mayor of Chicago Richard Daley, whose poops must be full of secrets. A suppository helps with hemorrhoids or constipation (or an anal dildo if you're really lonely) — to break up your shit. You want to use repository instead, which is a container that stores things. Thus, you can have a repository of poop, but not a suppository of information.

7. Saying it wrong: "Fall by the waste side"
Doing it right: "Fall by the wayside"

To "fall by the wayside" means that you aren't keeping up with a group, like in jogging. The person lagging behind in gym class during the mile (which was me) would have been "falling by the wayside." If they "fell by the waste side," they would have done so in a pile of trash. As if anything could have made gym worse.

8. Saying it wrong: "Circumvent the globe"

Doing it right: "Circumnavigate the globe"
The definition of "circumvent" is to "evade" or "go around," as in dodging an obstacle or problem. Thus, if you see your ex in public with their new boyfriend, you may want to circumvent that situation by walking another direction or turning the fuck around. You cannot, however, evade the Earth. You're on it.

9. Saying it wrong: "Self-depreciating"
Doing it right: "Self-deprecating"
Self-deprecating means to take oneself down or undervalue oneself, which makes it closely related to "depreciating," even if saying that version is wrong. "Depreciating" is an economic term used to indicate that the value of something drops over time, like Jessica Alba or Fred Durst's musical career. You can diminish your value (a face tattoo is a great place to start), but if you're using "self-depreciate" to make fun of yourself, you're diminishing your value in the wrong way.

10. Saying it wrong: "Irregardless"
Doing it right: "Regardless"
Just because Gretchen Weiners says it doesn't mean it's correct, even if it's a Mean Girls quote. "Ir" is a prefix that negates the phrase that comes before it, which is unnecessary when "less" is already doing the same thing. You could say "irregard," I suppose, but that also sounds stupid. "Irregardless" might not be in the rules of feminism, but it's the rules of English.

11. Saying it wrong: "Towards" / "Anyways"
Doing it right: "Toward" / "Anyway"
This is just an unnecessary "s" problem, which plagues many a word in the English language. "Towards" is a common British

version of "toward" but unless you are British (and if you are, call me), you shouldn't be using it. It's not an affectation (ala "favourite"); it's just not correct.

12. Saying it wrong: "Another thing coming"
Doing it right: "Another think coming"
Okay, I'll admit. This malapropism is infuriating, and the wrong version just sounds more right. The only way this makes sense is if you use the whole phrase as originally intended. The complete phrase goes "If that's what you think, you've got another think coming." Translated from stupid, this means that if you have an incorrect thought, you better think again. I don't like it, but here we are.

13. Saying it wrong: "Escape goat"
Doing it right: "Scapegoat"
For the record, like "doggy-dog world," I've never heard "escape goat" in real life, but I kind of love it. Where do I get an escape goat? Do they have wings? Can we reenact Chicken Run?

14. Saying it wrong: "Jive with"
Doing it right: "Jibe with"
I get where this comes from. When someone says they "jive with" something, they mean to indicate that they are "cool with it" or can "get down with it." This is similar to the actual phrase "jibe with," which means "to agree with." So, when Barack Obama says he believes in equal marriage, that all people should be able to have whatever state-sponsored lesbian commitment ceremony they choose, I "jibe with" that. But I don't "jive with" it. That's racist.

15. Saying it wrong: "Make due"
Doing it right: "Make do"

Literally, to "make due" would be to force something to be turned in at an appropriate time. If you were checking a book out from a library, the librarian on staff will make your selection due on a certain date. However, your librarian will likely be "making do" with the slashing of funding for education and the arts instead — or making the best of a situation. "Make do" is short for "make do well enough."

16. Saying it wrong: "All of my children" / "Outside of"
Doing it right: "All my children" / "Outside"

In such phrases, Americans have a tendency of inserting an extra "of," which is just not needed here. Think of our beloved Erica Kane, played by the seemingly ageless Susan Lucci. Did she lose a million Emmys acting in "All of My Children?" No. She lost them on "All My Children." Let soap opera be your guiding light through all things.

17. Saying it wrong: "Runner-ups"
Doing it right: "Runners-up"

There's a great exchange between Rory and Lorelai on Gilmore Girls where they argue over the plural of "cul-de-sac," which is "culs-de-sac." This makes Lorelai wonder whether other words can be pluralized in the middle, like "wheelsbarrow," and Rory explains that it's French. Next time someone asks you about "runners-up," I suggest you just say, "It's English."

18. Spelling it wrong: "Peak/peek my interest"
Doing it right: "Pique my interest"

This kind of makes sense, if you mean to say that your interest in something has reached its highest point. However, pique means to "provoke or arouse," which makes more sense in context. "Peek" just sounds creepy and wrong.

19. Spelling it wrong: "Scott free"
Doing it right: "Scot free"

I actually know someone named "Scott Free," and every time someone misspells it, I just think of him. Remember: You're not freeing our friend Scott over here. If you're getting off "scott free," you're getting away with something with few consequences, like our friend George Zimmerman.

20. Spelling it wrong: "Baited breath"
Doing it right: "Bated breath"

Were your breath "baited," that means that your breathing is currently being taunted or tormented, which could be true. I don't know your life. However, it's more likely that with "baited breath," you are waiting in suspense to learn the outcome of something. Don't bully your breaths. Let them live.

21. Spelling it wrong: "Without further adieu"
Doing it right: "Without further ado"

You can remember this as "without further interruption," which is what "ado" suggests. In the title "Much Ado About Nothing," Shakespeare wanted to suggest that the entire strife between Benedick and Beatrice is a lot of sound and fury signifying nothing. If he said "Much Adieu," they would just be saying goodbye a lot. That would have made for a very strange play.

22. Spelling it wrong: "Free reign"
Doing it right: "Free rein"

It's easy to see the misconception here. By saying "free reign," you want to indicate that a ruler or royal has the ability to do whatever (s)he pleases when it comes to their kingdom, having "free reign" over the land. But that's not what it's meant to indicate. "Free rein" comes from equestrian jargon, meaning to give your horse freedom of motion, holding loosely the reins to go easy on ol' Black Beauty.

23. Saying it wrong: "Hunger pains"
Doing it right: "Hunger pangs"

Like many phrases on this list, "hunger pains" is a perfectly sensible phrase to use, and anyone who has ever had to go on a religious fast knows the feeling of pain when you haven't eaten for 48 hours. To all my friends who fast for Ramadan every year, you're way more badass than I will ever be. However, hunger pangs is the original phrase, indicating the sharp jolts you feel from hunger. Yes, this is pain. I realize. No, I didn't not make up the English language.

24. Saying it wrong: "Step foot"
Doing it right: "Set foot"

"Step foot" isn't horribly wrong, and if the occupants of the house in The Conjuring said they would never "step foot in that home again," no one would notice the difference — just the demons. What you mean to say is that you would never again place one of your feet inside a haunted house (if you know what's good for you), meaning you would never "set" your foot inside it. Stepping your foot just sounds slightly awkward.

25. Saying it wrong: "Should of"
Doing it right: "Should have"

This is a mistake that people more often use in speech — less so in print. It's likely just due to vocal laziness and bad practice (personally, I can't say "get rid" to save my life) than a misunderstanding of how verbs work. "Of" is a preposition, not an auxiliary verb like "should."

26. Saying it wrong: "Wreck havoc"
Doing it right: "Wreak havoc"

To "wreck havoc" would mean the opposite of what the speaker intends. They mean to say that whomever is doing the wreaking is going on a "rampage of destruction," but wrecking it would mean to destroy it or thwart it. And who wants that? Instead use wreak meaning "to inflict."

27. Saying it wrong, sometimes: "Try and"
Doing it right: "Try to"

"And" is often used in place of a preposition after a verb, but the more appropriate version is to use "to" — in most cases. (Like almost every rule in the English language, it seems to get broken anyway — whenever English feels like it.) So if you're saying that you plan to "try and go to the park," that accidentally splits up your phrasing, making it sound like two different actions. They are not independent. You are doing the trying in order to go to the park. And why not? It's a beautiful day. Get outside.

28. Saying it wrong, sometimes: "Doing good"
Doing it right: "Doing well"

This depends on what you mean to say. If someone asks you how you are and you respond, "I'm good," this is incorrect. You need an adverb here, or else you mean that you embody the properties of goodness. Take if from Tracy Jordan: "Superman does good. You do well."

29. Saying it wrong: "Nipped in the butt"
Doing it right: "Nipped in the bud"

Okay, this is a good one, too. The verb "to nip" means to seize, to pinch or to bite. So if you want to nip something in the butt, you better be prepared to be slapped. However, if you want to "nip something in the bud," you're squashing it or taking care of it. Perhaps you are doing both? I don't know. I don't know your life.

30. Saying it wrong: "On accident"
Doing it right: "By accident"

This is one of those dumb English language things that makes me feel sorry for English language learners. You can do something "on purpose," but English doesn't allow you to do it "on accident." You do it "by accident," just like you don't do it "by purpose." That just sounds silly.

31. Saying it wrong: "Beckon call"
Doing it right: "Beck and call"

To be at someone's "beck and call" means to wait on them hand and foot or to be ready in case you are summoned. The word "beck," meaning a nod or some other signal that you're required, actually comes from "beckon," so it's not strange that "beckon call" ended up in parlance. It's intended to mean that you're being beckoned (or called) over. However, it's English. Just because it makes sense doesn't mean it's right.

32. Saying it wrong: "Safe haven"
Doing it right: "Haven"

"Safe haven" isn't really wrong. You can say it. It's just redundant. It would be like saying "scarlet red." Scarlet is already a form of red, so it's a little more explanation than you actually need. The definition of "haven" implies that it's safe already. The more alarming thing is if it were an unsafe haven, which would defeat the purpose and not be a haven at all.

33. Saying it wrong: "Mute point"
Doing it right: "Moot point"

A mute point would imply that the point were unable to articulate itself due to an impairment that leaves it speechless. Thus, unless your point is learning speech with Annie Sullivan, you have a "moot" point on your hands, a legal term dating back to the 16th century that means "open to debate."

34. Saying it wrong: "Case and point"
Doing it right: "Case in point"

The former would imply that your case and your point are two different things, a duo ala Mary and Rhoda. No offense to Mary Tyler Moore, but one would want to say "case in point," meaning that you are bringing up an example that proves what you are attempting to argue.

35. Saying it wrong: "Less than 140 characters"
Doing it right: "Fewer than 140 characters"

Sorry, Twitter users. When you want to keep those updates short, you want them to be "fewer than 140 characters." Fewer is used to refer to multiples of something, meaning that you hope Lebron scores "fewer" than 30 points in a game — or God doesn't exist. When you say "less," you're talking about a whole, one singular unit. If you're in salary negotiations with your boss and he gives you a smaller figure than you desire, it's less than what you wanted — not fewer.

36. Using it wrong: "Fit as a fiddle"
Say instead: "In good health"
If you're reading this, you're using this phrase wrong. Almost everyone gets it wrong — including yours truly. The real phrase "fit as a fiddle" means that something is "perfect" for its intended use — not "fit" meaning healthy but fit as in suitable or appropriate, like "fit for a king." So "fit as a fiddle" really means "as perfect as possible." The more you know.

37. Saying it wrong: "Old adage"
Doing it right: "Adage"
This is another redundancy thing. You can say "old adage;" you just don't really need to. The word "adage" already implies that the saying or phrase is old. (Have you ever said the phrase "new adage?") You can save yourself a syllable by just dropping the "old" altogether. And if you find one of them new adages, you let me know.

38. Saying it wrong: "Extract revenge"
Doing it right: "Exact revenge"
If you were "extracting" revenge, that means that you would be drilling the surface of the planet for it in order to burn for fossil fuel — and unless you're in a Tarantino movie, I don't think revenge works like that. According to our friends at Merriam-Webster, exact means to "to call for forcibly or urgently and obtain." So you could "exact" oil, especially if you're George W. Bush, but you cannot extract revenge.

39. Saying it wrong: "The spitting image"

Doing it right: "The spit and image"

To me, both versions of this phrase sound pretty silly. What images have you been spitting on recently? I'd prefer to keep my spit in my mouth — and I don't want to be compared to someone's spit. The original phrase "spit and image" comes from the Bible, where God made Adam out of "spit and mud" in order to make him in his own image. God didn't spit on him, as the modern idiom seems to suggest, but if you read the Old Testament, trust me, he could have done a lot worse.

40. Saying it wrong: "Mano a mano"
Doing it right: "Man to man"

For loyal viewers of Arrested Development, you know that adding an "o" to the end of things doesn't necessarily make them Spanish. If you wanted to say "man to man," you would say "hombre a hombre" — not hand to hand. "Mano a mano" may imply that you want to fight, instead of discuss things in person.

41. Saying it wrong: "Begging the question"
Doing it right: "Raising the question"

If you want to bring up a question you have on your mind, you shouldn't "beg" the question — because that means something very different. "Beg the question" is a term that indicates someone's argument has a conclusion that lacks adequate support from its premise. In order cases, this logical fallacy entails simply restating the premise instead of making an actual conclusion or having a conclusion that's totally unrelated to the initial. Welcome to every Freshman comp class.

42. Saying it wrong: "On tender hooks"
Doing it right: "On tenterhooks"

Where have you ever met a tender hook? I'm sorry, but even the gentlest hook is still pretty sharp. Hooks aren't exactly great cuddlers. Instead, "on tenterhooks" is used to indicate suspense — that you're waiting for something anxiously. A "tenterhook" is a type of hook used for drying cloth. I don't know how that's suspenseful, but maybe you're drying your laundry with Nathaniel Hawthorne.

43. Saying it wrong: "Near miss"
Doing it right: "Near hit"

If you break down the phrase "near miss," it doesn't make a lot of sense. If a car were to "nearly miss" another in an accident, that would tell you there was a collision. It almost missed, but then it didn't. A "near hit" would indicate instead that the cars nearly collided but evaded the crash at the last second. You'll never hear anyone say "near miss," including me, but there you go.

44. Saying it wrong: "Hone in"
Doing it right: "Home in"

In its classical use, the verb hone means to "sharpen with a whetstone," but in its modern sense, we often say that we are "honing" our skills — refining or perfecting them. This, then, has little to do with "honing in" on something, which means to focus your attention on an event, object or conversation — if you like to drop eaves. Instead, you would want to "home in" on it. It sounds silly, but then again, so do a lot of things that are technically correct.

Bonus: Saying it wrong: "One in the same"
Doing it right: "One and the same"

I want to think the best of you, internet, and that you already know this one, but here goes anyway. The phrase "one and the same" reemphasizes its phrasing to indicate that two things are exactly the same. You could just say "the same," but the "one" gives it an extra "oomph." One in the same would imply that thing is inside of itself, which to me, just sounds painful.

13

25 Things You Don't Have To Justify To Anyone

Chelsea Fagan

1. Your job. Yes, even if you're working something that other people condescendingly term "not a real job," such as retail or service. If you have a job of any kind in this economy, you've already won.

2. Whether or not you have debt. If you managed to get out of your education debt-free, that doesn't mean that your life is a financial walk in the park that you constantly have to be apologizing for. If you are in debt, it doesn't mean you got a "worthless" degree and now deserve to be shamed for struggling to find work after you were convinced by your school that you were making a good decision.

3. The kind of food you enjoy eating, or why you enjoy eating. (No matter how "uncultured" or "boring" or "gross" someone else might deem your favorite food.)

4. Your decision to have children, or not have them, or to not be sure if you even want them.

5. Your dislike for marriage as an institution — and even if this one day changes, you don't have to justify having grown as a person and moved into a new point of view. No one should be telling you "I told you so" over something as enormous as your decision to commit for life to another person.

6. Your sexuality, or your desire to experiment with it. You are allowed to have "phases" or "try things out" or be "confused," and can take as much time as you want figuring it out.

7. Your gender presentation.

8. Your income level, and what you can and cannot afford. If you are having trouble keeping up with friends because you are not able to spend as much as them, there is no reason to risk financial ruin to try and keep up appearances.

9. Your body. The only person whom you need to talk to about with it is your doctor; everyone else can else can go kick rocks.

10. Whether or not you want to go out on a weekend night, or ten weekend nights in a row. The amount of time you spend in a bar or at a club does not directly correlate with how cool or worthy a person you are.

11. Your relationship status. If you're single and happy, that's great. If you're in a relationship and happy, that's great. If you're either of those and not happy, you are

more than allowed to be, and it's no one's business how you should "fix" it unless you ask them for their advice.

12. How many friends you have. One is enough. A hundred is enough. And there is no need to falsely upgrade acquaintances to "friend" status in your mind simply to fill out the ranks. A true friend is rare, and we don't need to make it a competition for who has the most.

13. How much you drink when you go out, or if you drink at all, or why you choose not to drink if you do.

14. What kind of music you enjoy listening to.

15. What kind of an education you have or don't have, or if you intend to go back and finish what you've started. If continuing your studies is something you want to do, good, but don't be forced into saying that you want it just because it's what people expect of you.

16. What you happen to be turned on by. If you like slash fiction, you like slash fiction. If you like people recording videos of themselves popping balloons, that's awesome for you. It's all good, and as long as you're not hurting anyone, have at it.

17. Whether or not you know to cook, even if you're a woman who "should" know how to do those things.

18. If you stay at home to raise your children, or if you hire someone to help you do so because you have a full-time career. Neither of those choices are more or

less feminist, no matter what Elizabeth Wurtzel tells you.

19. How many people you have had sex with.

20. Whether or not you are a virgin, and whether or not you want to wait for marriage to lose said virginity.

21. Whether or not you believe in God, and what you think God actually is. (As long as you're not imposing any of your beliefs on others, in which case we'd have a bit of a problem. But I trust that you're cool and wouldn't do that.)

22. Who you voted for and why. If you want to talk about it, you're free to. But no one should ever make you feel like you have to tell them.

23. If you have sex on a first date, if you kiss on a first date, or if you won't even hold hands on a first date. You're allowed to do whatever you like when you've just met a new potential suitor.

24. Whether or not you choose to use dating websites.

25. Not knowing exactly what you want to be when you grow up, even if many people would already put you in the category of "grown up." If you are considering going back to school, or changing careers, or moving, or starting a family, or doing charity work — it's all good. And none of it has to be followed up with a longwinded explanation about why it's a good idea and they should believe in you. If you need to justify what makes you happy to someone in your life, perhaps

you should ask yourself why you even care about their opinion in the first place.

14

16 Tips For Being Cool At Parties

Ted Pillow

1. Follow any thematic guidelines provided by the people throwing the party — nobody likes someone who shows up empty-handed or out-of-costume. If it's BYOB, bring your own beer. If it's a toga party, wear a toga. If it's a search party, bring a flashlight and tempered expectations.

2. Everyone knows that if you go to prison, you need to show everyone you're tough and can take care of yourself right off the bat. Usually this is done by beating up the first guy who messes with you. Well, being cool at a party works the same way — you need to show how cool you are as soon as you walk in the door. One method is to show up already wasted, like "Who needs a party? I'm cool drug-addicted guy!" Another is to walk up to the coolest person already at the party and just do a really elaborate magic trick.

WARNING: Do not combine these two strategies. Drunken magic, while cool, can be very dangerous.

3. Don't start conversations with, "A/S/L?"

4. Don't bring your mom. Like, don't even let her wait in the car. But if you do, take my advice and remember to roll the windows down.

5. You know how you usually feel like sobbing during social gatherings because you feel so unmistakably alone? How you are inescapably struck by the futility of meaningful human connection? Uh, well, try not to feel that way anymore.

6. Bring a bottle of liquor and invite everyone to take shots with you. If you really want to be cool, don't even charge them full price.

7. Show up with a D-list celebrity. You could probably rent Alicia Silverstone or the lead singer of Smash Mouth for like $50 a night on Craigslist.

8. Try not to grunt as much as usual.

9. Bring a friend that's a minority of some sort. This shows that you're really worldly and have a diverse group of friends. Also, the rarer the minority the better, so if you show up with like an Eskimo or something, you're definitely getting laid. Only bring one minority friend though — what kind of party do you think this is?

10. Try not to draw any vivid parallels between the way people at a party carnally flaunt their bodies for the approval and gratification of others with the way that

meat is evaluated and packaged at a meat-processing facility.

11. Stand immediately outside a circle of good looking people having an engaging conversation rife with in-jokes. Listen long enough to craft your own joke about someone they've been talking about, or an experience that they've all shared. Use this as your opening, and then stand amidst their group with a pained, contorted facial expression for about 20 to 30 seconds.

12. Make plenty of topical references (i.e. a casual remark about the latest Rush Hour film).

13. Become really good at a drinking game that everyone else is playing. Unless the game is called "Hide in the Attic." Then they've tricked you again.

14. Go outside occasionally to smoke a cigarette. It's a good way to make friends, it makes you look cool, and you're already dead on the inside, anyway.

15. Pick the drunkest person there and make out with them, but make sure that the person you actually want to make out with sees it. Try to ignore the fact that the other person is only making out with you because you're the 2nd drunkest person there and they're also trying to get the attention of someone else. Also, they just puked in your mouth a little.

16. Just be louder than everyone else.

15

37 Questions

Dan Hoffman

1. Am I a masochist?
2. Do I know how to enjoy myself?
3. Do I like people? Yes, I like people, but how much?
4. Do I want a girlfriend?
5. If so, where are the girlfriends?
6. How is it supposed to feel when you like someone?
7. How many people do you have to have sex with before you find the one?
8. Should you have sex on the first date?
9. How many people regret having had sex with me?
10. Do people resent me in ways I can't imagine?
11. Am I damaged, romantically?
12. If so, can I be repaired, so to speak?
13. Are things as exciting as they should be?
14. Do I make enough effort to have a full, rich life?
15. What is a full, rich life?
16. Do I have convictions?
17. Do I get enough work done?

18. What are we to make of people who work in social media?
19. What does it mean to grow as a person, and am I growing?
20. If not, what should I do?
21. Does it mean you haven't "lived" if you stay in on the weekends?
22. Am I on the verge of understanding life and happiness in a new way?
23. Am I mature or immature?
24. When will something interesting happen?
25. Do I take myself seriously?
26. Will I have health insurance after I turn 26?
27. Do I have goals and ambitions?
28. If so, why am I bored?
29. I feel old. How is that possible?
30. What will I be like when I am 55?
31. Do I make too many excuses?
32. What are we to make of people who've actually suffered?
33. Should I take up yoga?
34. Am I sufficiently humble?
35. Am I likable?
36. Are people without college loans happier?
37. What has become of me?

16

23 Life Lessons You Get From Working At A Restaurant

Chelsea Fagan

1. If you don't have a thick skin and complete abandonment of political correctness, don't go near the kitchen. You will immediately learn there that what you consider to be off-limits is just the baseline of someone else's sense of humor.

2. Bad tippers are the worst kinds of people, and are often terrible in many other ways than just being cheap.

3. Correction, the worst people are those who don't tip or tip very badly, and accompany their financial insult with a snarky note left on the receipt.

4. The pain of a bad seating chart is a real one, and not a single customer will care or understand that you got slammed while someone else is totally dead.

5. The difference between the people who have never worked in food service, and the people who have, is always clearly visible. And a lot of time it has to do with the basic degree of respect they give to the people who are serving them.

6. Make back-of-house's life easy, they will make yours easy. Working is always about scratching someone's back so they'll scratch yours, and you'd better not break that chain.

7. The only people you're going to be able to hang out with — and often date — are by default going to be other people in the industry. So you better like the people you work with it, because no one else is going to be coming out with you at 1 AM.

8. There is absolutely zero shame in eating the plate that gets sent back barely-touched because someone either misunderstood what they were ordering or is incredibly fussy about their perfectly-good food. People who will judge you over shit like that are people who don't know the joys of a pristine plate of onion rings coming back to you when you are starving.

9. The most important friend you will make is the one who will cover for you while you eat, crouched next to some appliance in the kitchen. True friendship is about taking the fall so someone can eat.

10. There are a lot of people who are going to look down on you for working a restaurant, and treat you with massive disrespect, and you just have to get over it and remind yourself to never be like that in your own life.

11. If you are good to your server, your experience will be about a thousand times better, and you might even get free stuff if you're lucky.

12. There is nothing better than a chef who is currently trying out new stuff and has tons of excess food for everyone to try. The best friend anyone can have is a good chef.

13. Line cooks are some of the hardest-working, most humble and honest people in the working world. And many of them happen to be felons. And when you see them get off a 14-hour shift and still manage to make jokes with you at the end of it, you realize that every judgment we make about the guy with neck tattoos is completely off base.

14. If you're a female waitress/hostess/bartender, some of the more drunk male customers will take it upon themselves to also designate you "professional receiver of gross comments and inappropriate touches."

15. A good manager is the one who will shut shit like that down, because they would rather lose the money from that customer than have someone who mistreats their staff.

16. Even the best establishment can be run into the ground by a petty, spiteful manager.

17. There is no worse an experience on this planet than working a busy brunch shift when you are brutally hungover.

18. If you don't make friends with the bartender from

the get-go, your life is going to be difficult. And you quickly learn that this also applies to the places you don't work at — treat your bartender well, reap the rewards.

19. The calm before the storm (also known as the rush) is one of the most precious, fleeting moments in life. And as soon as you see that first customer looking at the specials board just a little too long, you know that it's already over.

20. Never be the person who comes in just as the kitchen's closing and orders something really complicated. Just don't be that person.

21. In the best restaurants, you'll become like a little family, and live through several very important moments together (especially because you don't get days off for normal, human things such as holidays or birthdays).

22. There will be one item on the menu that you fall in love with so much that you actually start having dreams about it, and go through withdrawal when you don't have it for a long enough stretch of time. You can actually get that way over, say, a cream of crab soup. It's like heroin.

23. Going back to a place you used to work and seeing all the old group — and getting to eat and drink all your favorites again — is one of the best feelings you can have.

17

7 Things To Do Before You Settle Down

Charlotte Green

1. **Date the wrong person.**
   Date that person who is way too old, way too young, or way too emotionally flakey to consider at any other time. Date someone who makes absolutely no sense, except for the fact that your whole body melts when they touch your hand while walking. Date someone simply because they turn you on and make you feel something, even though you know all too well that it's doomed to end before the end of the summer. Make that mistake and get the lust out of your system, because dating someone so clearly wrong for you is not a luxury we are often afforded.

2. **Have a fling.**
   Go somewhere for only a little while and fall in love with someone even though there is an expiration date on your romance from the day it starts. Have a tearful

goodbye at the airport and promise to keep calling each other. You'll stop calling each other after a few months, but that's how it was supposed to go. Don't feel badly.

3. **Work on a project that consumes your time.**
Do something you have always wanted to do but which doesn't enable you to have anything close to a social life, let alone a functional relationship. Throw yourself into the degree, the promotion, the internship, or the backpacking tour of Asia that you have always dreamed of doing but knew that you couldn't do if anyone else was depending on you. Let yourself take up all your time and not feel guilty about refusing to share it. Watch how many things can happen when you remove all distractions.

4. **Go on a vacation with a friend.**
Have some bonding that doesn't end in sex. Run wild on a town that neither of you two have been to before and make all of the ridiculous decisions you can only make when your friend — and not your lover or a family member — is by your side. Have one of those cliché-yet-wonderful bromance/girl crush excursions that result in a million photos to look back on with nostalgia and the kind of memories that neither of you can make when you're all tied up in a million different commitments.

5. **Get in shape just for you.**
Decide what you want your body to look like, work towards that goal every day, and don't let anyone distract you from the goals you have for your own

106

physique. Don't do it because you want to be sexier, or want the perfect beach body — at least, not if those are for anyone's eyes but your own. Focus entirely in proving to yourself that you can set yourself to something and follow through with it, and transforming the body you were convinced that you were stuck in forever. Make yourself perfect-looking to your own standards, and don't worry about what anyone else thinks of it.

6. **Learn how to orgasm really well.**
   Masturbate with every toy at the porn store. Watch every video your heart desires. Find out exactly what makes you orgasm, and do it. Over and over. Don't ever let anyone touch you in the wrong way again (especially not because you don't know how to direct them any more effectively.)

7. **Get your heart broken.**
   Feel what it is like to have absolutely no hope for your romantic future, to be totally alone in every sense of the word, and be completely numb to all of the supportive wishes of your well-meaning friends. Understand what it is to rebuild yourself bit by bit and to not really know if you're ever going to fall in love again until you actually do it. Because only once you've gone through it a first time can you ever be sure that you'd be able to do it another, if push came to shove. And who knows — even when you're "settled down," you just might need to do it again.

18

5 Self-Help Books That Actually Helped

David Cain

There's something about self-help that is fundamentally uncool. Being into coin-collecting or Dungeons & Dragons is an order of magnitude more socially acceptable than having titles like "How to Get People to Like You" and "You Can Be Happy No Matter What!" staring out from your bookshelf.

Somehow it isn't yet obvious that a persistent interest in self-improvement is probably the defining trait of the interesting and accomplished person. Self-help literature, though, is a particular kind of self-improvement. Turning to self-help is admitting you don't quite know how to drive a regular human life. It's like designating yourself with a voluntary "special needs" status.

I don't think the need for some intentional re-balancing is special though. None of us are born knowing how to drive. It's probably not unusual to feel like you've never been taught quite how to steer a human life competently, but it may be unusual to admit.

I think what makes us most suspicious of self-help is that we've all seen people who are constantly absorbing it and not changing a thing. There are self-help junkies out there — people who get high on the feeling that their life is improving simply by reading the book, yet never actually address their habits in everyday life. They get high on the feeling of possibility, and when the feeling fades they buy another.

Their mistake is simple: they're missing the "self" part of self-help. Insights by themselves are useless without action, which is what changes lives. But you can get the self-help high just by reading, and that high is enough to make you feel (for the moment) that nothing needs fixing.

The self-help junkie habit is obvious and ugly to everyone else, and so the whole genre is reviled for its empty promises, rather than the reader for his total lack of responsibility. Consequently, self-help remains so uncool that even hipsters won't touch it.

Another reason these books are uncool is that most of them are crap. They tend to be written by psychologists who know a lot about what's wrong with the reader but don't have much in the way of charisma or writing chops, which makes the reading experience dry and kind of embarrassing. Their examples are cheesy and long-winded. Aside from being boring and clinical, they're often just dorks.

There are gems though. Some of them, for me, were pivotal in developing in me a much freer and lighter way of moving through the world. Incorporating the bits that moved me and ignoring the rest, they helped me form a worldview that actually suits the world the way it is, and lets me live in it in a way where joy is normal and angst is the exception. So they should be read without shame.

The big ones:

1) *Don't Sweat the Small Stuff (…and it's all small stuff)* – Richard Carlson

I was nearing my own rock bottom around ten years ago when a family member lent me this book. I was struggling in college. I had no self-esteem, a small and shrinking circle of friends, and couldn't imagine how things could get better. I read it in a couple of bus commutes, and I could feel things lightening.

The whole book is 100 short strategies for dealing with day-to-day stresses and downers. Each one is about a page.

"#22: Repeat to yourself, "Life isn't an emergency." #4: Be aware of the snowball effect of your thinking. #40: When in doubt about whose turn it is to take out the trash, go ahead and take it out. #76: Get comfortable not knowing."

It was my first exposure to the incredible leverage a person has by learning how to let life happen and respond calmly, rather than trying desperately to control what happens.

Since then I've noticed that that's the basic difference between happy people and sad people: the happy people concern themselves with what they can do on their end. Sad people concern themselves with everything else.

Anyone could benefit from this book.

2) *Wherever You Go There You Are* – Jon Kabat-Zinn

Jon Kabat-Zinn is a stress management expert who has found

that the most powerful tool for dealing with daily stress is mindfulness.

Wherever You Go There You Are amounts to an elegant introduction to informal meditation, but a person could get a lot out of it even if they have no intention of ever sitting cross-legged with closed eyes. You can feel your mind slowing down as you read the rough-cut recycled pages, its short passages intercut with Kabir and Rumi verses. Kabat-Zinn keeps it non-denominational and fluff-free.

If you spend a decade reading different people's accounts of how to be happy, you discover that almost all of them can be boiled down to a few principles, and the primary one by far is to keep your attention in the present moment. That's what mindfulness is. It is an art, and there may not be a gentler and more readable introduction to it than this book.

If you do check it out, and you like the tree he's barking up, his later (and much larger) book Coming To Our Senses takes an even deeper look at mindfulness in real life.

3) *The Four Agreements* – Don Miguel Ruiz

In The Four Agreements, Don Miguel Ruiz characterizes personal beliefs as agreements, which is right on the mark; nothing is true to you unless you agree that it is. If, in your eyes, you're no good, you have agreed at some point that you are no good. You will live this truth until you stop agreeing. We typically don't realize we're constantly making these agreements, yet they define your personal world, which is the only world you'll ever live in.

Ruiz advocates identifying and challenging all the agreements you've accumulated, and toss them out in favor of agreeing to four commitments:

Be impeccable with your word, don't take anything personally, don't make assumptions, and always do your best.

If you make those agreements it's almost impossible to let yourself down, feel guilt or give in to fear. They short-circuit virtually all self-defeating human behaviors.

These days, rather than trying to be perfect each day with each agreement, I work the agreements backward when things seem to be going wrong. Anytime I feel stuck, it takes about five seconds to identify which of the four agreements I broke to get there. Either I've been untruthful in some way, I'm making assumptions, I'm taking something personally, or I'm cutting corners. I don't know if I've ever gotten myself into trouble in any way other than those.

4) *The Power of Now* – Eckhart Tolle

Oprah made him simultaneously popular and uncool in most demographics when she did a whole webseries on A New Earth, the follow-up to The Power of Now. He was attacked by the religious housewife contingent of Oprah's audience for his "false religion," which is all nonsense if you read *A New Earth* or its predecessor — they're both nonreligious and straightforward. And he's an extremely nice man.

The Power of Now is an exceptional book. It's easy to recognize the primacy of living in the moment as an ingredient to happiness, and Eckhart Tolle is by no means the first to focus on it. But he goes further by articulating that it is not only the only path to happiness, but the entirety of the path — there's nothing else you need to do, because all of our suffering comes from living in thoughts about a badly-remembered past or an imaginary future.

The concept is ancient, and Tolle credits the ancients for it, but he's one of the first to deliver it in plain language with no religious coloring or mythological allegories. He just tells you how to do it.

5) *This is How* – Augusten Burroughs

If you still can't get over your self-help gag reflex, then this is the one for you. Augusten Borroughs set out to write a self-helpful book that derides certain self-help standards — particularly the catch-all prescription of positive thinking to everyone when many help-seekers are people who are experiencing extreme suffering and suicidal thoughts.

A lot of self-help is rather generalized, for people who feel troubled but not quite maimed by serious instances of loss or abuse. Burroughs has had a difficult life, which he shares candidly in This is How, addressing his fellow sufferers of the worst baggage imaginable. The subtitle of the book is Help for the self: proven aid in overcoming shyness, grief, molestation, disease, fatness, lushery, spinsterhood, decrepitude and more, for young and old alike.

He really digs into the ugliness of personal suffering and tells you how to deal. Some of the chapter titles give a clue: How to Feel Like Shit, How to Be Fat, How to Get Over Your Addiction to the Past, How to End Your Life, How to Lose Someone You Love, How to Let a Child Die.

The tone is very different from traditional self-help. There's no smileyness or pandering. Burroughs is blunt and a bit foul-mouthed, and tells you what's going to work and what isn't, if you really do want to get better. The result is refreshing. You feel like you're being slapped and told how it is, rather than being hugged and told to think happy thoughts.

*****

The way self-help works is by the adding up of poignant bits over time. Reading a great book like one of these can give you the feeling of breaking through in real-time, and it may even leave you different forever. But there are no cures — the rest of your life will always remain ahead of you, so it's a matter of becoming better equipped to manage it.

Your natural skepticism and fluff-detector will dismiss a lot of what you read, and this is good, but certain aphorisms and skills will stick. Once in a while one will appear in your mind at exactly the right time, and you feel yourself doing something differently. And now a window is open where you didn't know there was one. Your world has gotten a bit bigger, and a bit lighter.

THOUGHT
CATALOG
Books

Thought Catalog Books is a publishing house owned by The Thought & Expression Company, an independent media group based in Brooklyn, NY. Founded in 2010, we are committed to facilitating thought and expression. We exist to help people become better communicators and listeners in order to engender a more exciting, attentive, and imaginative world.

Visit us on the web at
www.thoughtcatalogbooks.com and *www.collective.world.*

Made in United States
Orlando, FL
13 July 2024

48937616R00075